Rulers of India

HARSHA

D1880787

Owing to the antiquity and rarity of this book, certain pages are regrettably absent, and readability is compromised due to the blurring of the original text. If you possess any insights regarding the availability of these missing sections, kindly inform us. Your assistance is crucial in ensuring the completion of this significant work for the benefit of future generations.

Rulers of India

HARSHA

BY

RADHAKUMUD MOOKERJI

GYAN

Published by

Gyan Publishing House
5, Ansari Road
Daryaganj, New Delhi-110002
Phone: 011-47034999, 9811692060
E-mail: books@gyanbooks.com

Distribution Network
gyanbooks.com
India, USA, Canada, UK, Australia

© Publisher

All rights reserved. No part of this work may be reproduced, stored, adapted, or transmitted in any form or by any means, electronic, mechanical, photocopying, micro-filming, recording or otherwise, or translated in any language, without the prior written permission of the copyright owner and the publisher.

ISBN: 978-93-6208-075-2 (PB)
First Published, 1926

2nd Impression 2024

Printed at: Gyan Press, Delhi.

The book is sold subject to the condition that it shall not, by way of trade or otherwise, be lent, resold, hired out, or otherwise circulated without the prior publisher's written consent.

RULERS OF INDIA HARSHA
Author: RADHAKUMUD MOOKERJI

Rulers of India

HARSHA

By the same author

A HISTORY OF INDIAN SHIPPING

LOCAL GOVERNMENT IN ANCIENT INDIA

THE FUNDAMENTAL UNITY OF INDIA

NATIONALISM IN HINDU CULTURE

MEN AND THOUGHT IN ANCIENT INDIA

ETC.

THE COINS OF HARṢA

From the casts kindly supplied by Mr. Prayag Dayal,
Curator, Provincial Museum, Lucknow)

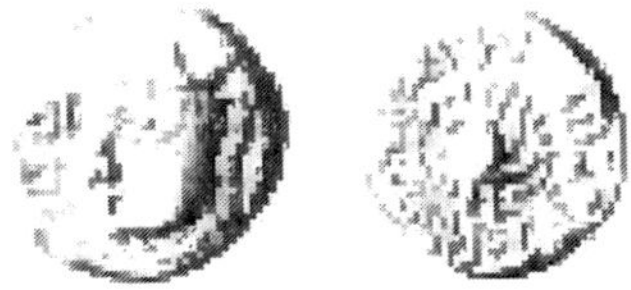

No. 1

Obverse.

Head of king to *l.*; crescent with knobs at crown of head.

To left of head ·

·Sa' and date 1?

cf *JRAS* 1906, p. 846. No. 1

Reverse.

Peacock standing facing with head to *l.*, wings and tail outspread. Head of peacock to *l.*

Legend :

. . ni-r ava-ni-pa-ti-Srī-śa-la.

No. 2

Obverse.

As on No 1. Crescent nearer crown.

·Sa' and date 6?

JRAS. ibid.. No. 2.

Reverse.

As on No. 1. Parts of full legend which is :

Ji-vi-tā-va-ni-r ava-ni pa-ti-śrī
sa-la-da-tya-di vam ja-ya-ti.

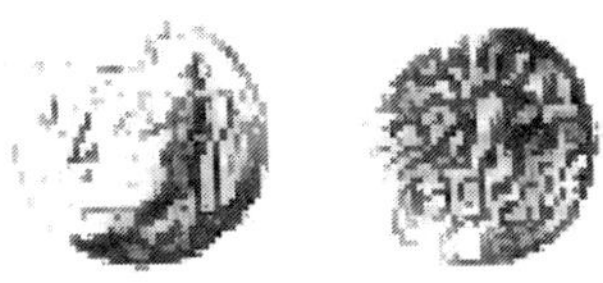

No 3

Obverse.

As on No. 1 Crescent at crown of head. Date illegible.

JRAS, 1906, Pl. No. 9.

Reverse.

As on No. 1.

Head of peacock to left.

Legend :

Vi-ji-tā-vani-r....... ha-r-śa ?

HARSHA

(Calcutta University Readership Lectures, 1925)

BY

RADHAKUMUD MOOKERJI
M.A., Ph.D., Itihāsa-Śiromaṇi
PROFESSOR AND HEAD OF THE DEPARTMENT OF INDIAN HISTORY, LUCKNOW UNIVERSITY
HIS HIGHNESS SIR SAYAJI RAO GAEKWAD MEDALLIST, PRIZEMAN, & LECTURER
1925–30

OXFORD UNIVERSITY PRESS
LONDON: HUMPHREY MILFORD
1926

TO

THE MEMORY OF

SIR ASUTOSH MOOKERJEE

FOR HIS UNIQUE SERVICES

TO THE CAUSE OF LEARNING AND RESEARCH

AS VICE-CHANCELLOR, CALCUTTA UNIVERSITY

PREFACE

THERE are very few among the Rulers of India whose history is so rich in both contents and materials as the history of Harṣa. 'When all sources are utilized,' as observed by the late Dr. Vincent A. Smith, 'our knowledge of the events of the reign of Harṣa far surpasses in precision that which we possess respecting any other early Indian king, except Chandragupta Maurya, and Aśoka. Indeed, the historical material is so abundant that it would be easy to write a large volume devoted solely to his reign.'

His early life and career form the subject-matter of the *Harṣa-charita* of Bāṇa, a writer of great repute in the history of classical Sanskrit, who wrote on Harṣa as his court poet from his personal and intimate knowledge of his life and rule, and has given to Sanskrit literature one of its very few biographical works. Thus in Bāṇa Harṣa found his Boswell; but, though the historical value of the work as a whole is somewhat vitiated by its occasional outbursts of hero-worship and flights of fancy, to which a poet laureate's panegyric on his royal patron naturally lends itself, the line between fact and fiction is easily discernible, and the kernel of truth separated from its envelope of embellishments and exaggerations. And on the facts that are thus extracted, or narrated as such, Bāṇa's accuracy is surprisingly established by several specific and significant confirmations from other sources, all of which have been pointed out in the text. Moreover, it is to his poetical gifts that we owe some very real and valuable history in the graphic pictures they call up of the life of those days at different levels, in its different aspects and phases—the simple life of the lowly in the village, the busy and strenuous life of the camp, the high life of luxury and conventions at the court and the palace, or the ascetic and austere life at the hermitage. These descriptions of the manners, customs, and habits of the people of all ranks, and of the conditions of education and learning, culture and religion, of the times are not the least important and interesting part of history, for they enable us to realize the civilization of the age. What we thus lack of political history is amply compensated by what we get of social history in the *Harṣa-charita*.

The India of Harṣa is also described by another eye-witness, the famous Chinese pilgrim, Yuan Chwang, to whose account, which reads like a Gazetteer in the scope of its inquiry and its wealth of details, the history of ancient India perhaps owes more than to any other individual source for the reconstruction of some of its lost chapters. To add to these two unique sources, the reliable records of first-hand observation, we have several inscriptions of Harṣa himself, a few of his great contemporary, Pulakeśin II of the Deccan, and the larger body of inscriptions of the Gupta and later kings of northern India, which together throw considerable light on the history of Harṣa, especially on the interesting but imperfectly explored topic of the administrative system developed in that glorious age for the successful governance of extensive empires.

I am grateful to the Calcutta University for kindly asking me to deliver a Course of Readership Lectures embodied in this volume. My Lectures to my own post-graduate students at the Lucknow University have also expedited the preparation of the work.

The system of transliteration adopted here will be apparent from the following examples: Kṛiṣṇa, Lichchhavi, and Vaṁśa.

RADHAKUMUD MOOKERJI.

THE UNIVERSITY,
LUCKNOW,
September 1925.

CONTENTS

Illustrations

CHAPTER I

EARLY LIFE AND ACCESSION

HARṢA[1] is one of the few examples in our ancient annals of a king who by his conquests made himself a king of kings and achieved the political unification of a large part of India as its paramount sovereign. The principal source of his history is the *Harṣa-charita*, the *Life of Harṣa*, by Bāṇa, one of the Court poets of the Emperor Harṣa. This indigenous literary evidence is copiously supplemented and corroborated by the evidence of the famous Chinese traveller, Yuan Chwang, who has recorded his first-hand observations of what he saw of the emperor's life and work.

There are also three known inscriptions of Harṣa which supply some very valuable information: these are the Sonpat Copper Seal (No. 52 in Fleet's *Gupta Inscriptions*), the Banskhera plate of year 22 of

[1] Sometimes called Srī Harṣa without much justification. The *Śrī* was not a part of his name; otherwise we should have the form *Śrī Śrī Harṣa* which occurs nowhere. In the Kauṭhem grant of Vikramāditya V, he is called *Harṣa-mahānṛipa* [*IA*, xvi, 22], while Bāṇa's work is called simply *Harṣa-charita* [Fleet, *Gupta Inscriptions*, p. 207, n. 3]. Some inscriptions call him *Harṣa-deva* [e.g. the Nausārī grant and the Aphsad Stone Inscription (*IA*, xiii, 73, 79)], a name also occurring in the *Harṣa-charita*.

Harṣa era, i.e., of about A.D. 628, and the Madhuban plate of year 25 or A.D. 631. But the information derivable from these inscriptions directly bearing on Harṣa is importantly supplemented by the entire body of the inscriptions of the age beginning with those of the imperial Guptas, especially on the interesting subject of the administrative system of the times.

The founder of the house was Puṣpabhūti, a devoted worshipper of Śiva, who came under the influence of a noted Śaiva saint of the Deccan, Bhairavāchārya by name. Once the king is said to have followed his guru to a cremation ground for purposes of Tāntrika worship and won from his deity the boon that he would be 'the founder of a mighty line of kings' [*HC.*[1] 109–27].

The Madhuban Plate Inscription gives the names of the immediate ancestors of Harṣa as follows:

Naravardhana *m.* Vajriṇīdevī
|
Rājyavardhana I *m.* Apsarodevī
|
Ādityavardhana *m.* Mahāsenaguptādevī
|
Prabhākaravardhana (Mahārājādhirāja) *m.* Yaśomatī (daughter of Emperor Yaśodharman Vikramāditya of Mālava).

[1] The translation of *Harṣa-charita* by Cowell and Thomas has been mainly used for the citations from Bāṇa.

Text of the Banskhera Copper-plate Inscription

1 Śrī svasti Mahānauhastyaśvajayaskandhāvārāchchhrīvarddhamāna-
koṭyā mahārājaśrīNaravarddhanastasya puttrastatpādānudhyātaśśrī-
Vajriṇīdevyāmutpannaḥ paramādityabhakto mahārājaśrīRājyava-
rddhanastasya puttrastatpādānu-

2 dhyātaśśrīmadApsarodevyāmutpannaḥ paramādityabhakto mahārā-
jaśrīmadĀdityavarddhanastasya puttrastatpādānudhyātaśśrīMahāse-
naguptādevyāmutpannaśchatussamudrātikkrāntakīrttiḥ pratāpānu-
rāgopa-

3 natānyarājo varṇṇāśramavyavasthāpanapravṛittachakkra ekachakkra-
ratha iva prajānāmārttiharaḥ paramādityabhaktaḥ paramabhaṭṭā-
rakamahārājādhirājaśrīPra[bhā]kara[va]rddha[na]styasya puttrasta-
tpā[dā]-

4 nudhyātassitayaśaḥ pratānavichchhuritasakalabhuvanamaṇḍalaḥ pa-
rigṛihītaDhanadaVaruṇEndraprabhṛitilokapālatejāssatpathopārjjitā-
nekadraviṇa bhūmipradānasaṁprīṇitārthihṛdayo-

5 tiśayitapūrvvarājacharito devyāmamalayaśomatyā(ṁ) śrīYaśomatyā-
mutpannaḥ paramaSaugatassugata iva parahitaikarataḥ parama-
bhaṭṭārakamahārājādhirājaśrīRājyavarddhanaḥ । rājāno yudhi du-

6 ṣṭavājina iva śrīDevaguptādayaḥkṛitvā yena kaśāprahāravimu-
khāssarvve samaṁ saṁyatāḥ । utkhāya dviṣato vijitya vasu-
dhāñkṛitvā prajānāṁ priyaṁ prāṇānujjhitavānarātibhavane satyā-
nurodhena yaḥ । tasyā

7 nujastatpādānudhyātaḥ paramamāheśvaro Maheśvara iva sarvvasat-
vānukampo paramabhaṭṭārakamahārājādhirājaśrīHarṣaḥ Ahichch-
hattrābhuktā VaṅgadīyavaiṣayikapaśchimapathakasambaddhaMark-
kaṭasā-

8 gare samupagatānmahāsāmantamahārājadaussādhasādhanikapramā-
tārarājasthānīyakumārāmātyoparikaviṣayapatibhaṭachāṭasevakādīn-
prativāsijānapadāṃścha samājñāpayati viditama

9 stu yathāyamuparilikhitagrāmassvasīmāparyantassodraṅgassarvva-
rājakulābhāvyapratyāyasametassarvvaparihṛitaparihāro viṣayādud-
dhṛitapiṇḍaḥ putrapauttrānugaśchandrārkkakṣitisamakā-

10 līno bhūmichchhidranyāyena mayā pituḥ paramabhaṭṭāraka-
mahārājādhirājaśrīPrabhākaravarddhanadevasya māturbhaṭṭārikā-
mahādevīrājñīśrīYaśomatīdevyā jyeṣṭhabhrātṛiparamabhaṭṭāraka-

11 MahārājādhirājaŚrīRājyavarddhanadevapādānāñcha puṇyayaśobhi-
vṛiddhaye Bharadvājasagotrabahvṛichachchhandogasabrahmachāri-
bhaṭṭaBālachandra-Bhadrasvāmibhyāṁ pratigrahadharmaṇāgrahāra-
tvena pratipā-

12 dito viditvā bhavadbhissamanumantavyaḥ prativāsijānapadaira-
pyājñāśravaṇavidheyair bhūtvā yathāsamuchitatulyameyabhāga-
bhōgakarahiraṇyādipratyāyā etayorevopaneyāssevopāsthāna[ñcha]
ka-

13 raṇīyamityapi cha । Asmatkulakkramamudāramudāharadbhiranyai-
ścha dānamidamabhyanumodanīyaṁ । Lakṣmyāstaḍitsalilabud-
budachañchalāyā dānaṃ phalaṃ parayaśaḥ paripālanañcha ।
Karmmaṇā ma-

14 nasā vāchā karttavyaṁ prāṇibhi(r)hitaṁ. Harṣeṇaitatsamākhyāta-
ndharmmārjjanamanuttamaṁ [।*] Dūtakotra mahāpramātāramahā-
sāmanta Śrī Skandaguptaḥ Mahākṣapaṭalādhikaraṇādhikṛitamahāsā-
mantama

15 hārāja[Bhāna]samādeśādutkīrṇṇaṁ

16 Īśvareṇedamiti samvat 20 2

17 Kārti vadi 1 [।।*]

18 SVAHASTO MAMA MAHĀRĀJĀDHIRĀJAŚRĪHARṢASYA.

THE BANSKHERA INSCRIPTION

In the account of Bāna, Harṣa's father, Prabhākaravardhana, beginning as a petty chief of a 'district called Sthāṇviśvara in the land of Śrīkaṇṭha', very nearly attains the position of an emperor by subduing or overawing a number of countries and peoples all over northern India He became 'a lion to the *Huṇa* deer, a burning fever to the king of the *Indus land*, a troubler of the sleep of *Gujarat*, a bilious plague to that scent-elephant the lord of *Gāndhāra*, a looter to the lawlessness of the *Lāṭs*, an axe to the creeper of *Malwa's* glory' [*HC.* 133]. 'Levelling on every side hills and hollows, clumps and forests, trees and grass, thickets and ant-hills, mountains and caves, the broad paths of his armies seemed to portion out the earth for the support of his dependants' [*ibid.*]. Thus he became 'famed far and wide under a second name, Pratāpaśīla'. In the inscriptions also he is described as 'one whose fame spread beyond the four seas, and to whom submitted the other kings in power or love' [Madhuban Plate] and is given the title of 'Mahārājādhirāja Paramabhaṭṭāraka', whereas his father Ādityavardhana, and grandfather Rājyavardhana I, are simply called Mahārājās.

About the year A.D. 590,[1] Queen Yaśovatī or Yaśomatī (according to the Sonpat Seal Inscription) gave birth to Harṣa 'in the month Jyaiṣṭha, on the twelfth day of the dark fortnight, the Pleiads being in the ascendant, just after the twilight time'. The birth of the prince was announced to the king by

[1] See Note B to Ch II, showing how these dates are arrived at.

Suyātrā, the daughter of the queen's nurse. When Prince Rājyavardhana was nearly six years old, his sister Rājyaśrī was born, about the year A. D. 593. At that time Harṣa was old enough only 'to manage five or six paces with the support of his nurse's fingers', and 'tiny teeth were beginning to adorn his mouth', as Bāṇa informs us (115, 116), so that he could not be more than two years old at the most. As the royal children began to grow up, their maternal uncle, Queen Yaśovatī's brother,[1] deputed his son Bhaṇḍi to serve the young princes. Later on, the king appointed as their companions the two sons of the Malwa[2] king, who were also their uncles [Note A, Ch. II], viz. Kumāragupta and Mādhavagupta [*HC.* 154]. This probably shows that the Malwa king was subordinate to him.

Not many details are given of the education of the princes.[3] They grew up 'adamantine in the hardness of their frames', 'borne on horses and well-proportioned like Aruṇa and Garuḍa', with their hands daily begrimed with the marks of sword-play, while their

[1] Emperor Śīlāditya of Mālava, son of Yaśodharman Vikramāditya; as explained in Note A, Ch. II, he deputed his son to the Court of Thanesar under terms of a treaty forced on him by his defeat by King Prabhākara. This event took place about A. D. 593.

[2] i. e. Eastern Malwa as distinguished from Mālava proper under Emperor Yaśodharman (A. D. 533–83), and his son and successor, Śīlāditya (A. D. 583–93; A. D. 604–6), as explained in Note A, Ch. II.

[3] Bāṇa furnishes the information, hardly noticed, that Harṣa had a third brother named Kṛiṣṇa (59), while he also credits Harṣa himself with a son (101).

recreation time was marked by the deep twang of their bows (151).

Their sister Rājyaśrī 'gradually grew up in daily increasing familiarity with friends expert in song, dance, &c., and with all accomplishments' (156). 'In a comparatively limited period she came to maturity' and was given away in marriage to Prince Grahavarman, son of King Avantivarman of the royal house of the Mukharas[1] (156), with due pomp and ceremony: 'even kings girt up their loins, and busied themselves in carrying out decorative work set as tasks by their sovereign', while 'from the farthest orient came the queens of all the feudatories'.

After some time, his old enemies, the Hūṇas,[2] again began to create trouble, but the king was too old to take action himself. So he summoned to his presence his eldest son, Rājyavardhana, 'whose age now fitted him for wearing armour, and, as a lion dispatches his

[1] The Harāhā Inscription [*Ep. Ind.* xiv, p. 110] connects this dynasty with the Solar race and mentions as its founder King Aśvapati of the Madras, the father of Satī Sāvitrī of the *Mahābhārata*. The antiquity of the family is historically demonstrated by the fact that on a clay seal discovered at Gayā appears in the Mauryan Brāhmī characters the legend *Mokhaliśa* = Maukhareḥ [Fleet, *Gupta Inscriptions*, p. 14]. The term *Mukhara* is cited in the *Kāśikā* as an example of *Gotrāvayara*, i.e. insignificant gotras, kulas, or families, from which the formation *Maukharyā* is derived under Pāṇini, iv. 1, 79.

[2] The Aphsad Inscription of Ādityasena refers to the Maukharis of Kanauj being also troubled by, and chastising, the Hūṇas. Thus both the kingdoms of Kanauj and Thanesar must have been united as allies against their common enemy, the Hūṇas. The cause of this alliance is explained in Note A, Ch. II.

whelp against the deer, placed him at the head of an immense force and sent him attended by ancient advisers and devoted feudatories towards the north to attack the Hūṇas' (166). Harṣa, then too young to be associated with this commission, would not, however, be left behind, but followed his brother with a cavalry force. While his elder brother was hunting out the enemy in the hills, Harṣa engaged himself in hunting down 'the lions, śarabhas, tigers, and boars' plentiful in the forests at the foot of the hills. 'His bow drawn to the ear, he emitted a rain of shining shafts which in a comparatively few days left the forests empty of wild creatures' (167).

While the two brothers were thus engaged, the messenger Kuraṅgaka came from the capital to Harṣa with a letter conveying news of his father's serious illness, 'a violent fever'. Instantly Harṣa rode away back to the capital and did not take any food for three days until he found himself at his father's bedside. Among the physicians in attendance on the king are mentioned Suṣeṇa (171), and Rasāyana who had mastered the Āyurveda in all its eight divisions (177), while, passing on through the third court of the

[1] It is interesting to note that the Chinese traveller, I-tsing, who visited India shortly after Yuan Chwang, also mentions the eight divisions of the Āyurveda of the times which he describes as treating respectively of (1) sores, inward and outward; (2) diseases above the neck, and (3) below the neck, i.e., bodily diseases; (4) demoniac diseases due to attack of evil spirits; (5) antidotes to poisons; (6) diseases of the children from the embryo stage to the sixteenth year; (7) the means of lengthening life; and (8) the methods of invigorating the legs and body.

palace, the prince perceived the smell of boiling oil. butter, and decoctions used in preparing medicines for the sick king. On arrival at the palace, Harṣa dispatched express couriers and swift camel-riders one after another for fetching his elder brother, but in the meanwhile King Prabhākaravardhana died. His parting words to Prince Harṣa were: 'Succeed to this world; appropriate my treasury; make prize of the feudatory kings; support the burden of royalty; protect the people; guard well your dependants; practise yourself in arms; annihilate your foes'[1] (188). A monument in brick was set up on the sepulchral pile of the dead king, while Harṣa 'with longing heart awaited his brother's advent' (195).

Rājyavardhana at last returns, with 'long white bandages bound about arrow wounds received in battle while conquering the Hūṇas' (197), and was so much affected by his father's death that he resolved to renounce the world and turn an ascetic, leaving the throne to his younger brother. But Harṣa was too noble-hearted to accept this position, and forced the throne on his brother by his compelling arguments and attitude.

But the throne did not mean any peace to either of the ill-fated brothers. Suddenly, a distinguished

[1] It is not clear whether these words indicate the king's preference of Harṣa for the throne in supersession of the claims of his eldest son who was away. Such nominations by kings of their successors were not, however, unusual in those days, as shown in some of the Gupta inscriptions cited below.

servant of Princess Rājyaśrī, Saṃvādaka by name, brought to the new king the tidings of a grave calamity: 'On the very day on which the king's death was rumoured, His Majesty Grahavarman was by the wicked lord of Mālwa[1] cut off from the living along with his noble deeds. Rājyaśrī also, the princess, has been confined like a brigand's wife with a pair of iron fetters kissing her feet, and cast into prison at Kānyakubja.[2] There is moreover a report that the villain, deeming the army leaderless, purposes to invade and seize this country as well. Such are my tidings: the matter is now in the king's hands' (204). At this news, Rājyavardhana's grief yielded to a more violent passion, and, in a paroxysm of wrath, he burst out:

[1] i.e. Śīlāditya, with whom was also associated Devagupta, king of eastern Malwa (mentioned in the Madhuban Plate Inscription). See Note A, Ch. II.

[2] From this sentence has been inferred the fact that the Maukhari kingdom was Kanauj. There is also another passage in the *Harṣacharita* (254) describing Kanauj as being a Maukhari city which had been seized by the Gupta king of Malwa [Guptanāmnācha gṛihīte Kuśasthale (i. e., Kanauj)] before Rājyaśrī was imprisoned there. It is, however, possible, and there are some who take this view, that Kanauj, where Rājyaśrī was kept in prison by the Malwa king, was a part of *his* dominion. That the Maukharis were *not* rulers of Kanauj is also supposed from the fact that their inscriptions were all found far away from Kanauj, in Magadha (Bihar Province). Against this, however, is to be considered the *provenance* of their coins which were all found associated with the coins of Śīlāditya (Harṣa) and Prātāpaśīla (Prabhākara) in a place near Kanauj—the Fyzabad district. Dr. Mark Collins (in his *Geographical Data of Raghuvaṁśa* and *Daśakumāracharita*) suggests the compromise that, while Avantivarman and Grahavarman were kings of Kanauj, the original Maukhari kingdom was probably Aṅga.

'Mālwas to maltreat the race of Puṣpabhūti!—this is the hind clutching the lion's mane, the frog slapping the cobra, the calf taking the tiger captive!' and delivered the following instruction to Harṣa: 'Let all the kings and elephants stay with you. Only Bhaṇḍi[1] here must follow me with some ten thousand horse'. So saying, he ordered the marching drum instantly to sound. But Harṣa, not less excited over the incident, could not easily reconcile himself to his brother's order to remain behind, and earnestly entreated his brother to revoke it. He pleaded that he need not stay for the sake of keeping control over the feudatories, who were all 'secured by the bonds of his virtues', and argued: 'If you think it inopportune that two should go, gratify me with the commission'. In the end, he sank his head to the ground and fell at his brother's feet, till he was upraised and consoled by his brother, saying: 'A concourse of lions in the

[1] We thus find Bhaṇḍi going to fight against his father. But this circumstance would not appear to be very strange in view of the estrangement that had inevitably grown up between father and son during a long period of separation. We must recall that Bhaṇḍi was sent away by his father to a foreign court in A. D. 593, when he was a boy of only eight years of age, and was treated there by King Prabhākara as a 'third son' (*HC*, 117), and by his own sons as 'a fourth brother' (*ibid.*). It is not surprising that this affection under which Bhaṇḍi was being brought up in a foreign court for about twelve years overcame that for his natural father!

We may also note in this connexion that Bhaṇḍi is also mentioned by Yuan Chwang as one of the leading figures of Harṣa's court under the name *Bāṇi*. This is one of those vital confirmations which have established the historicity of Bāṇa's narrative.

matter of a deer is too degrading. Be pleased to stay'. Thus kept back, Harṣa 'could scarcely make the time pass, alone as he was like a wild elephant strayed from the herd' (204–8).

Very soon it was Harṣa's turn to be confronted single-handed by a more serious calamity. One day, when in the audience chamber, he noticed Kuntala, a chief officer of cavalry, and a favourite of his brother, entering in haste with a dejected company, to deliver to him the heart-rending news that 'his brother, though he had routed the Mālwa army with ridiculous ease, had been allured to confidence by false civilities on the part of the king of Gauḍa, and then, weaponless, confiding, and alone, dispatched in his own quarters' (208). The king of Gauḍa[1] was, according to the evidence of Yuan Chwang, 'Śaśāṅka, the wicked king of Karṇasuvarṇa in East India, a persecutor of Buddhism' [Watters' translation, i. 343], who uprooted the Bodhi tree [*Life*, p. 171]. The inscription gives the following account of the incident: 'He in battle curbed Devagupta and all

[1] According to one MS. of the *Śrī Harṣa-charita*, he is called Narendragupta [see *Ep. Ind.*, vol. i, p. 70], but according to the commentator on the *Harṣa-charita* he is named Śaśāṅka [see Bombay edition 1892, p. 195]. The translators of the *Harṣa-charita* very ingeniously find in the word *Śaśāṅka-maṇḍalam* a veiled allusion to King Śaśāṅka. This Śaśāṅka is identified with the Śaśāṅkarāja of a copper-plate inscription of the Gupta-samvat 300 (i.e., A.D. 619–20) who in that case must thus have reigned at least thirteen years after the murder of Rājyavardhana and the accession of Harṣa [see *Ep. Ind.*, vol. vi, p. 143]. Harṣa might then have shown a Buddhist's forgiveness to his brother's murderer or was not able to bring him to book. See Note C, Chap. II.

the other kings together and uprooted his adversaries; then he, through his trust in promises (*satyānurodhena*), lost his life in the enemy's quarters.' It thus admirably confirms the account of Bāṇa. The commentator on *Harṣa-charita* has stated that Śaśāṅka threw Rājya off his guard by his offer to marry his daughter to him as a token of his submission and friendship. But perhaps the real motive of the murder was inspired by the Machiavellian political maxim that 'if a frontier country has a virtuous ruler, this is the unhappiness of the mother kingdom!' [Beal, i. 210].[1]

At this point in the life of Harṣa, Yuan Chwang interposes some interesting facts not fully mentioned by Bāṇa. According to the Chinese pilgrim, when the throne of Kanauj fell vacant on the death of King Rājyavardhana, 'the statesmen of Kanauj, on the advice of their leading man Bāṇi, invited Harṣavardhana, the younger brother of the murdered king, to become their sovereign. The prince modestly made excuses, and seemed unwilling to comply with their request', until his hesitation was removed by the

[1] In the *Gauḍarājamālā*, Mr. A. K. Maitra makes the novel suggestion that Rājya died in an open conflict with Śaśāṅka. He cites passages from the *Harṣa-charita* (cited here also) to show that after his easy defeat of the Malwa king, Rājya put Bhaṇḍi in charge of the spoils of the victory, and himself proceeded to Kanauj with a reduced force, only to find himself overwhelmed by the much superior force with which the Malwa king's ally, Śaśāṅka, had come all the way from his kingdom in Bengal to help him in the conquest of Kanauj. Thus Rājya had to surrender to Śaśāṅka, who did not consider it prudent to spare his life.

Bodhisattva Avalokiteśvara, who 'promised him secret help, but warned him not to occupy the actual throne and not to use the title Mahārāja. Thereupon Harṣa-vardhana became king of Kanauj with the title Rājaputra and the style Śilāditya' [*ibid.*]. In the *Harṣa-charita*, however, which gives a somewhat different[1] version of this episode, the Bodhisattva is replaced by 'the goddess of Royal Prosperity who took him in her arms and, seizing him by all the royal marks on all his limbs, forced him, however reluctant, to mount the throne—and this though he

[1] According to Bāṇa, it was rather the old Commander-in-chief, Siṁhanāda, than Bhaṇḍi who was concerned with Harṣa's accession to the throne. The latter was away from the capital when Rājyavardhana died, for he had accompanied him in his campaign against Malwa from which he returns victorious only to meet Harṣa on the way among the Vindhyas where he was wandering in search of his sister. On the whole, as we shall see, Bāṇa, as an historian, is sometimes more reliable than the Chinese pilgrim.

It may also be further noted that while Yuan Chwang mentions the hesitation of Harṣa to occupy the vacant throne, Bāṇa knows of no such hesitation. C. V. Vaidya [*Mediaeval Hindu India*, vol. i, p. 7] thinks that here also Bāṇa is right, and that the hesitation referred to was in respect of the throne of Kanauj, and *not* of Thanesar with which it is confused by the Chinese traveller. The widowed Princess Rājyaśrī was the lawful heir to the throne of Kanauj on the demise, without leaving any male issue, of her husband Grahavarman. Thus Harṣa could not possibly agree to misappropriate and 'occupy the throne of Kanauj', but preferred rather to rule 'in conjunction with his widowed sister', as stated in the Chinese work cited below. Thus there seems to have been an amalgamation of the two kingdoms of Kanauj and Thanesar under Harṣa, who now treated Kanauj as his head-quarters more than any other place in his empire. It may further be supposed that there was a combination of the military forces of the two kingdoms, which naturally helped Harṣa in his *Digvijaya*.

had taken a vow of austerity and did not swerve from his vow' (79). We have no means of ascertaining what this vow of austerity exactly was. Watters takes it to mean that Harṣa 'in the early part of his life had joined the Buddhist church and perhaps taken the vows of a bhikṣu, or at least of a lay member of the Communion'. But, according to Bāṇa, Harṣa became an adherent of Buddhism only after the completion of his extensive conquests (288). As regards the suggestion that he did not occupy the actual throne, we may consider the statement contained in the Chinese work *Fung-chih* that he administered the government in conjunction with his widowed sister [Watters, i. 345].

CHAPTER II

Campaigns, Conquests, and Suzerainty

A double task now confronted the youthful king: the recovery of his sister and the punishment of his brother's murderers. The news of this double calamity upset Harṣa so much that 'like Janamejaya he became intent on burning all sovereigns' (209), while the Senāpati, Siṁhanāda, a friend of his father, added fuel to his fire by saying: 'Think not of the Gauḍa king alone: so deal that for the future no other follow his example', and egged him on by calling up the example of Paraśu-Rāma, who, to avenge his father's death, 'one and twenty times cut down and eradicated the united power of the Kṣatriya race' (215). Harṣa responds to this call of his old commander-in-chief with equal enthusiasm: 'By the dust of my honoured lord's feet I swear that, unless in a limited number of days I clear this earth of Gauḍas, and make it resound with fetters on the feet of all kings who are incited to insolence by the elasticity of their bows, then will I hurl my sinful self, like a moth, into an oil-fed flame' (218). So saying 'he gave instructions to Avanti, the supreme minister of war and peace' that a proclamation should be engraved to the following effect: 'Let all kings prepare their hands to give tribute, or grasp swords; to seize the realms of space, or chowries; let them bend their heads, or their bows, grace their ears with my commands, or their bowstrings, crown their heads with the dust of my feet, or with helmets'.

Then the emperor summoned to his presence Skandagupta,[1] the commandant of his whole elephant troop, and asked him to call in the elephant herds out at pasture (222), 'commanding his march for a world-wide conquest' (225). In obeying his master's orders, Skandagupta, like the Senāpati, did not forgo his right to admonish the youthful king. Said he: 'Loyal devotion requires of me a few words. . . . The story of His Majesty Rājyavardhana has given you some inkling into the despicable characters of vile men. Thus do national types vary, like the dress, features, food, and pursuits of countries, village by village, town by town, district by district, continent by continent, and clime by clime. Dismiss, therefore, this universal confidingness so agreeable to the habits of your own land and springing from innate frankness of spirit. Of disasters due to mistaken carelessness, frequent reports come daily to your Majesty's hearing'. He then gave to Harṣa a long list of such disasters, mostly from legends, but

[1] This official's name is also mentioned in two inscriptions, Nos. 528, 529 in Kielhorn's List. This is a remarkable proof of the trustworthiness of Bāṇa's work as a source of history.

in a few cases from history, such as that of the Maurya king Bṛihadratha slain unawares by his own general Puṣpamitra. Thus the idea of a regular *digvijaya* was urged on Harṣa by all his officers in their loyalty to the best interests of his house. He was further encouraged in his conquests by the spirit of the subordinate princes accompanying him, who, in their war-fever, thus mapped out the field of their aggression: 'The land of the Turukṣas is to the brave but a cubit. Persia is only a span. The Śaka realm but a rabbit's track. In the Pāriyātra country, incapable of returning a blow, a gentle march alone is needed. The Deckhan is easily won at the price of valour' (240). As we shall see, this threat was not completely realized, especially that about the Deccan, which administered to the emperor the greatest rebuff of his life!

Then on an auspicious day in which was 'fixed an hour of marching suitable for the subjugation of all the four quarters' (227), the king accompanied by his kinsmen (*kulaputras*) and feudatories (*sāmantas*) 'issued forth from his house, like the Golden Foetus from Brahma's egg, to set on foot an age of gold'. His first halt on the march was near the Sarasvatī, whence he came to Kathaka where he was visited by a confidential messenger, Haṁsavega by name, who had been sent to him by the new and young sovereign of Assam, Bhāskaravarman, with costly presents and proposal of an alliance[1] which was accepted by him.

[1] According to some historians, their alliance was a long-standing one. It was sought by Kāmarūpa as a protection against the

Then dismissing Haṁsavega 'with a load of answering gifts in charge of eminent envoys', he continued to 'advance by ceaseless marches against the foe until one day he heard from a letter-carrier that Bhaṇḍi had arrived with the Malwa king's whole force, conquered by the might of Rājyavardhana's arm, and was encamped quite near'. Soon Bhaṇḍi came in sight with a single horse and a retinue of a few nobles, and related to Harṣa the whole story of his brother's death in full, and, on the king asking what was his sister's plight, said: 'Your Majesty, I learnt from common talk that after His Majesty Rājyavardhana was taken to paradise and Kanyākubja was seized by the man named Gupta, Queen Rājyaśrī burst from her confinement and with her train entered the Vindhya forest' (254). Then, inspecting the Malwa king's army and the booty captured and brought by Bhaṇḍi, which comprised 'thousands of elephants, horses, ornaments of divers kinds, yak-tail chowries, regal paraphernalia such as lion thrones, couches and settees, treasure chests with written records of their contents, and all the Mālwa king's adherents with their feet restrained by iron fetters',

enmity of the Guptas of Magadha, one of whom, Mahāsenagupta, defeated a king named Susthitavarman [Aphsad Stone Inscription, No. 42 of Fleet], who is supposed to be a predecessor of King Bhāskaravarman of Kāmarūpa. But it is more probable from the context of the epigraphic passage that this Susthitavarman was only a namesake of the Kāmarūpa king and was really a *Maukhari*, the ancestor of Avantivarman and Grahavarman of Kanauj. This was the view of Fleet [*Gupta Inscriptions*, Introduction, p. 15], which I see no ground for changing. See Note A to Ch. II, below.

and appointing overseers to take charge of the booty, the king, accompanied by the Mālwa prince, Mādhavagupta, and tributary kings, set out with the horse in search of his sister, and in a comparatively few days march reached the Vindhya forest. There Harṣa comes across Vyāghraketu, son of the tributary chief Sarabhaketu,[1] who introduces to him, as one familiar with every creek and corner of the hills, Nirghāta, nephew of the Vindhyan chief, Bhūkampa by name. Nirghāta refers Harṣa to a mendicant of the name of Divākaramitra whom the king identifies as a former friend of his sister's husband. Originally a follower of Vedic religion and of the Maitrāyaṇī Śākhā, he turned a Buddhist and had his hermitage in the Vindhyan forests, which soon grew up to be a great centre of learning and religion, attracting students of different sects and communities. On the king relating to him the cause of his coming, one of the mendicants informed him that he had seen in the morning a young lady in despair mounting the funeral pile, surrounded by a troop of other women, and said further that he had himself come in haste to his

[1] We probably owe to this acquaintance of Harṣa with a forest chief his introduction, in his drama of *Priyadarśikā*, of the character called Vindhyaketu, the king of the Āṭavikas or Foresters, who is also associated with the heroine Priyadarśikā as her protector in distress, just as in real life Harṣa's sister, Rājyaśrī, becomes associated with the Vindhyan chiefs in her distress. The plot of Harṣa's drama must have been suggested by the romances of his eventful life! The name Vindhyaketu is itself suggested by the names of the actual Vindhyan chief, Sarabhaketu, with his son, Vyāghraketu.

teacher that he might intervene and prevent the lady from committing her contemplated suicide. Harṣa, very much agitated at this information, implored the mendicant to show him where she was at once, and went on foot after him with all his tributary kings as well as the saint Divākaramitra. Following up some piteous cries, he was able to find his way to Rājyaśrī, then 'fainting as she prepared to enter the funeral pile', and pressed her forehead with his hand. At that reviving touch she recovered from her swoon and recognized her brother, who tried to comfort her by covering her mouth with his hands. On overcoming her emotion she allowed her brother to lead her away from the fire and sat down at the foot of a tree close by (280). In the meanwhile Divākaramitra had water brought by one of his disciples, with which the brother and the sister refreshed themselves, and then Harṣa said to his sister: 'My child, salute this holy man. He was your husband's second heart and is our guru'. Divākaramitra then presented the king with a pearl-wreath which he bound on his shoulder as an antidote to poison, whereupon the king reciprocated his kindness by saying: 'This body of mine is placed unreservedly at your disposal till death. You are now absolutely free to do with it what you please'. Rājyaśrī, who felt more attracted to the saint as her husband's friend, thus expressed her devotion: 'Your Holiness' coming stopped my resolution to die, even on the point of accomplishment; let me therefore in my misfortunes be allowed to assume the red robe' (285). But the saint, not accepting her downright devotion, as being the outcome of a temporary emotion, dissuaded her by saying that she must act as her lawful guardian, her brother, now, as her guru or father, desires. Harṣa said he could yield to her wishes subject to the condition that he must be permitted to cherish her for a while as his dearly loved sister lost and recovered, and must also be allowed time to carry out his own righteous vow of vengeance against his enemies. 'When I have accomplished my design,' the king said further, 'she and I will assume the red garments together'[1] (288).

On the accomplishment of that design the king now concentrated all his attention, energy, and resources. The series of troubles he had to face in his early life only burnt into his soul the supreme necessity for him of annihilating the system of things which could produce, or make possible, such troubles, the system[2] of too many small states in a condition of unstable political equilibrium, as well as of reviving and realizing the long-lost and traditional Kṣatriya ideal for a king to

[1] At this point, so early in his career, ends the *Harṣa-charita*, with the return of Harṣa and Rājyaśrī to Kathaka, the place from which he had set out in search of his lost sister.

[2] The existence of small states and of wars between them is also assumed by Harṣa in his dramas, *Ratnāvalī* and *Priyadarśikā*. The latter describes a war between Aṅga and Kaliṅga, between Kauśāmbī and Kaliṅga, and between Kauśāmbī and the Vindhyan state, while the former mentions a war between Kauśāmbī and Kosala whose king took shelter in a fort in the Vindhyas, supposed to have been within his dominion.

bring the whole country, as far as possible, under the 'umbrella' of one authority. Thus Rājaputra Śīlāditya launched forth his scheme of Digvijaya (the conquest of the quarters), for which he got together a large army comprising 5,000 elephants, 20,000 cavalry, and 50,000 infantry, but not including any chariots, which he probably condemned as useless. The details of his conquests are not fully available. According to Yuan Chwang, he first 'proceeded eastwards, invaded the states which had refused allegiance, and waged incessant warfare until in six years he had brought the five Indias[1] under allegiance' [Watters, i. 343]. But we have no details even about the most important of Harṣa's campaigns, that against the Gauḍa king, which supplied the motive of his digvijaya. Bāṇa only tells us that Harṣa put Bhaṇḍi in charge of that campaign, pending his quest of his sister, which he is more concerned to describe. He makes an indirect allusion to the campaign in a passage (200) where he speaks of 'the rise of the blotted moon, Śaśāṅka', as symbolizing the rising power of the Gauḍa king, of the 'red sunset' as indicative of bloody wars, and 'the buzzing bees' of arrows. In another passage (238) we are told of

[1] The 'Five Indias' are stated to be Svarāṣṭra (Panjab), Kānyakubja, Gauḍa (Bengal), Mithilā (Dārbhāngā), and Orissa. That Orissa was part of Harṣa's empire is indicated by the fact recorded in the *Life* (p 154), that Harṣa wanted to assign the revenue of eighty large towns of Orissa to Jayasena, the Master of the Śāstras, who was too spiritually minded to accept the royal favour.

'riders intently occupied in rehearsing the approaching Gauḍa war (*āgāmi-Gauḍa vigraham*)', but nothing as to how that approaching war was fought and with what results! From Bāṇa we gather further that Harṣa had 'pounded (*pramathya*) a king of Sindh', and 'taken tribute from an inaccessible land[1] of snowy mountains' (which may mean Nepal) (100–1), while the king of Assam sought his alliance at the very beginning. In the West his conquests included the kingdom of Valabhī. At first 'the lord of Valabhī, who had been defeated by the great lord, the illustrious Harṣadeva', sought the protection of Dadda II, the Gurjara king who belonged to the political system of the South under its paramount sovereign, Pulakeśin II the Chalukya,[2] but later he got back his kingdom as a vassal of Harṣa and even his son-in-law. As such he appears in the train of his father-in-law at the assemblies held by Harṣa at Kanauj and Prayāga which will be described later [Grant of Dadda of Bharoch and other epigraphs noticed in the *Indian Antiquary*, xiii. 70]. The name of this son-in-law of Harṣa is given as Dhruvasena (Dhruvabhaṭṭa) II [Watters, ii. 246]. His campaigns in Western India seem to have resulted in the submission to his

[1] M. Ettinghausen [*Harsha-Vardhana*, p. 47], supposes this land to be a Tukhāra country. The expression used by Bāṇa is: 'atra parameśvareṇa tuṣāra śailabhuvo durgāyā gṛihītaḥ karaḥ'.

[2] The Aihole inscription of Pulakeśin II [*Ep. Ind.*, vol. vi, p. 10] states how, 'subdued by his splendour, the Lāṭas, Mālavas and Gurjaras became as it were teachers of how feudatories, subdued by force, ought to behave'.

suzerainty of a few other states like those of Ānandapura, Ki-ta or (?) Cutch, and Su-la-cha or Suraṭha (Surat), all of which on the eve of Yuan Chwang's visit were regarded as dependencies of Mo-la-po,[1] or Western Mālava, formerly subject to Valabhī.[2] Some historians hold that Harṣa's conquests or political influence extended also to Nepal, from the assumption that his era was in use there [Bhagwanlal Indraji and Bühler in *IA*, xiv, p. 420], but this is denied by S. Levi, who points out that Nepal at that time was a dependency of Tibet, which, after Harṣa's death, helped Nepal in supporting the Chinese envoy Wang-hiuen-tse in his expedition against the usurper of Harṣa's throne.[3]

[1] According to Yuan Chwang, sixty years before his visit Mo-la-po was ruled by a great king named Śilāditya, identified by S. Levi with the Buddhist Śīlāditya I, surnamed Dharmāditya, of the Valabhī dynasty. The pilgrim also saw Dhruvabhaṭṭa reign in Valabhī as the nephew of Śīlāditya. Thus the inference may be made that Śilāditya Dharmāditya was also the original ruler of Valabhī to which he annexed Mo-la-po. The defeat by Harṣa of Dhruvabhaṭṭa resulted in the submission of both these territories to the suzerainty of Harṣa.

[2] The conquest of Valabhī justified the anticipation of Harṣa's royal companions that 'in the Pāriyātra (modern Aravallis) country, incapable of returning a blow, a gentle march alone is needed' (Bāṇa already cited). It is not certain, however, which country is meant by Bāṇa by this name, whether Valabhī or some other part of Rajputana. Yuan Chwang refers to a country he calls Pāryātra, which is identified by Reinaud with Bairāt, of which the king was more military than religious [Watters, i. 300].

[3] The evidence for Harṣa's conquest of Nepal is given as follows. Yuan Chwang mentions, as 'a recent king' of Nepal, Aṁsuvarman, whose inscriptions are dated Samvat 34, 39, and 45. It is believed that the era used by Aṁsuvarman (and in the other later Nepal

The only failure in his otherwise unbroken career of military success was that connected with his expedition to the south. As stated by Yuan Chwang [Watters, ii. 239], 'the great king Śīlāditya at this time was invading east and west and countries far and near were giving in allegiance to him, but *Mo-ha-la-cha* (i. e. Mahārāṣṭra) refused to become subject to him' under its great king Pulakeśin II, who made

inscriptions Nos. 9–15), is that of Srī Harṣa which begins in A. D. 606–7, and not his own, because in his own and some other inscriptions he is described as a mere *sāmanta* or a *mahāsāmanta*, a great feudal chief, under some other overlord. That the Harṣa era was in widest use in Northern India is testified to by Alberuni. No other era can meet the requirements of the case. There is further a definite statement in the Vaṁśāvalīs of Nepal that just before Aṁsuvarman's accession to the throne Vikramāditya came to Nepal and established his era there. Though the name Vikramāditya and the era mentioned here are wrong, the statement probably points to Harṣa's invasion of Nepal and to its result, the adoption of his era. V. A. Smith [*Early History of India*, 3rd ed., p. 341 n.] accepts the theory of Harṣa's conquest of Nepal against Sylvain Levi. The difficulty that Aṁsuvarman's inscription dated 34 Harṣa Samvat shows that he was living in A. D. 640 while Yuan Chwang, who was in India between 637 and 642, refers to him as a recent king, may be explained away by the consideration that the pilgrim's was only hearsay evidence, because he did not himself visit Nepal. That the Harṣa era was used in Nepal may be inferred from the Nepal inscriptions dated 113 and 119 of Śiva Deva, who, according to another inscription (No. 153 of Jayadeva), married the grand-daughter of Ādityasena whose father, Mādhavagupta, is mentioned as a contemporary of Harṣa in the Aphsad Inscription [see *Gupta Inscriptions*]. Now Ādityasena lived about A. D. 672 (cf. Shāhpur Inscription, *ibid.*), and if we take his time to be fifty years earlier than his grand-daughter (Vatsadevī by name), his grandson-in-law, Śiva Deva, should have lived about A. D. 720, and thus his inscriptions dated 113 and 119 can have a reference only to the Harṣa era to give that time for his life [see also K. M. Panikkar's *Śrī Harṣa* on this point].

himself the Lord Paramount of the south by his extensive conquests rivalling those of Harṣa in the north. That the two emperors met in actual fight is also stated in the *Life* of Yuan Chwang: 'Śīlāditya rājā, boasting of his skill and the invariable success of his generals, filled with confidence himself, marched at the head of his troops to contend with this prince but he was unable to prevail or subjugate him' [Beal, p. 147], although 'he has gathered troops from the five Indies and the best generals from all countries'. Probably this conflict was brought on by the aggression of Harṣa, who, after vanquishing Dhruvasena II, king of Valabhī, felt tempted to extend his conquests still further and try conclusions with Pulakeśin II, whose dominions he had to invade in the course of his conquests running smooth and uninterrupted so long. But little did Harṣa realize that on the other side of the Vindhyas there was a foeman worthy of his steel who, by his extensive conquests fully rivalling those of Harṣa, had become powerful enough to repel his invasion.

The Chinese pilgrim's account of this great conflict between the two paramount sovereigns of northern and southern India is also corroborated by the evidence of inscriptions. Thus in the Aihole inscription of A.D. 634, in which the poet Ravikīrti describes the exploits of his patron Pulakeśin II, there is a reference to that event in the following passage: 'Harṣa, whose lotus-feet were arrayed with the rays of the jewels of the diadems of hosts of feudatories prosperous with unmeasured might, through Pulakeśin had his joy (*harṣa*) melted away by fear, having become loathsome with his rows of lordly elephants fallen in battle'.[1] Another verse (24th) in the same inscription shows that the scene of the battle must have been somewhere about the Vindhya and the banks of the Rēvā (Narmadā), forming the northern limits of the empire of Pulakeśin, where his 'broad armies' were encamped and had checked the progress of Harṣa [see Fleet's *Dynasties of the Kanarese Districts*, p. 350]. There are also several inscriptions in which Pulakeśin is described as defeating the glorious Śrī-Harṣa, the lord of the whole northern country, in consequence of which he acquired the second title of Parameśvara[2] [Inscriptions nos. 401 and 404 in *Ep. Ind.*, vol. v, Kielhorn's List and p. 202, and in *IA*, vi. 87, viii. 244, ix. 125, and xi. 68, in all of which the formula used is: samarasaṁsakta sakalottarāpatheśvara Śrī Harṣavardhanaparājayopalabddha parameśvarāparanāmadheyaḥ]. Another inscription refers to 'Pulakeśi-Vallabha, who by the strength of his own arm had subdued the united strength of all hostile kings' [Nausārī plates of Śryāśraya Śīlāditya in *Ep. Ind.* viii. 230], while another describes him as 'acquiring the banner of victory in battle with Harṣavardhana, the lord of the region of the north' [*IA*, xiii. 74].

[1] 'patita gajendrānīkavībhatsa bhūto bhayavigalita harṣo yena chākāri Harṣaḥ.'

[2] According to the Haidarabad grant of A. D. 612, this title was acquired by Pulakeśin 'by defeating hostile kings who had applied themselves (or a hostile king who had applied himself) to the contest of a hundred battles' [Fleet, *Dynasties*, p. 351 n.].

The military success of Pulakeśin was due to the character of his people and of his administration, which are thus described by the Chinese traveller [Watters, ii. 239]: 'The inhabitants were proud-spirited and warlike, grateful for favours and revengeful for wrongs, self-sacrificing towards suppliants in distress and sanguinary to death with any one who treated them insultingly. Their martial heroes who led the van of the army in battle went into conflict intoxicated, and their war-elephants were also made drunk before an engagement. Relying on the strength of his heroes and elephants the king treated neighbouring countries with contempt . . . The benevolent sway of this king reached far and wide'. Indeed, his influence and reputation were not confined to India. According to an Arabic chronicle, in the 36th year of the reign of Khosru II of Persia (i.e. about A. D. 625), letters and presents were exchanged between him and the Indian monarch; while a painting in one of the caves at Ajantā probably points to this fact in showing the presentation of a letter from a Persian to an Indian king [*JRAS*, N.S., xi, pp. 157, 165–7].

Thus for a time the suzerainty of India was practically divided between two persons, Harṣa and Pulakeśin.[1] According to the Chinese traveller, when his wars and conquests were over, Harṣa placed his army

[1] The Yekkeri inscription of Pulakeśin II [*Ep. Ind.* v, p. 8], definitely calls him Dakṣiṇāpathapṛithivyāḥ svāmī, i. e. Lord of the whole country of the region of the south.

on a peace footing by making it overwhelmingly large and strong against the aggressive designs of the states subdued. He brought his elephant corps (which had enabled Pulakeśin to achieve his great victory over him) up to 60,000 and the cavalry to 100,000, and with such a force he was able 'to reign in peace for thirty years without raising a weapon'[1]

[1] This statement of Yuan Chwang may be considered along with his other statement, that Harṣa 'waged incessant warfare until in *six* years he had brought the Five Indias under allegiance', in fixing the dates of Harṣa's reign and conquests. As remarked by Watters, 'it is against text and context to make him represent the king as fighting continuously for thirty or thirty-six years'. Considering that in about A.D. 642 the king told the Chinese pilgrim that 'he had been lord of India for thirty years and more' [*Life*, p. 183], we may assume that all his conquests were over by about A.D. 612 and that he had become king six years earlier (the period of his conquests) in A.D. 606, the year 1 of the Harṣa era. This assumption is also strengthened by the fact that the quinquennial assembly held in the spring of A.D. 644 was the sixth held in his reign [Beal, *Life*, p. 184]. It is thus reasonable to conclude with Fleet, and against Vincent Smith [*Early History*, p. 340, n.], that Harṣa's wars with Valabhī and Pulakeśin took place within A.D. 612. Fleet's argument is based on the Haidarabad grant of A.D. 612, showing that Pulakeśin had then already established himself at Bādāmi, and hence this consolidation of his power must have been subsequent to his earlier expeditions and successes (including the defeat of Harṣa) described in the Aihole inscription of A.D. 634. The Haidarabad grant, though it does not mention Harṣa by name, implies, by the title which Pulakeśin acquired by his victory over him, that that victory had then already been achieved [Fleet, *Dynasties*, pp. 351 and 356]. It need not, however, be assumed from this that Harṣa, as the ruler of an extensive empire, could be entirely free from the necessity of further military expeditions. Even as late as A.D. 643 we find him returning from a successful campaign in distant Koṅgoda (Ganjām), where his great rival Śaśāṅka was recognized as

[Watters, ii. 343]. Thus his empire rested ultimately upon the basis of physical force.

We may now try to indicate the full extent of the empire under the direct and actual administration of Harṣa as distinguished from the extent of his influence. The sphere of authority is, of course, less extensive than the 'sphere of influence' or suzerainty. But in the records of the times, direct rule is sometimes confused with the power and authority indirectly exercised over a larger area by a paramount sovereign or a king of kings. What adds to the confusion is that these old empires were not organized as centralized administrations or unitary states, but were always compatible with, and, indeed, largely made up of, any number of local kingdoms acknowledging the suzerainty of a paramount sovereign such as Harṣa undoubtedly was in his age. Thus the problem of defining the extent of the old Indian empires is a problem connected with the peculiar lines on which Hindu political development generally proceeded. We know, besides, of many an instance in ancient Indian history of a great *Digvijayī* or conqueror like a Samudragupta reinstating vanquished kings in their

suzerain up to at least A. D. 619 [see Note C to this chapter]. Nor do we know how long he was engaged in trying to overcome Śaśāṅka himself. Further, we learn from the Aihole Inscription of Pulakeśin II, that he, too, had conquered both Kośala and Kaliṅga, and might thus have come into conflict with Harṣa in that region, which was evidently a storm-centre in that age. This assumption is made by Mr. R. D. Banerji [*History of Bengal* in Bengali, 2nd ed., p. 109].

kingdoms when they acknowledged his overlordship and offered to remain as his friends and allies, with obligations to follow their overlord in his wars or help him in other ways. Thus the king of kings builds up a political system of his own, a *maṇḍula*, as it is called in the Hindu political treatises, the 'sphere' or circle of states of which he is the centre[1] or paramount sovereign.

Firstly, then, as regards the territories directly administered and controlled by Harṣa, they are to be gathered not only from his own acquisitions and annexations by conquest, but also from those of his predecessors. From the words used by Bāṇa, it may be inferred that Harṣa's father, Mahārājādhirāja Prabhākara Vardhana, had by his conquests made his power felt in several distant countries, in Gāndhāra, the Indus land, the country of the Hūṇas, in Malwa, in Gujarāt, and the land of the Lāṭas. But we are not sure whether this meant the actual annexation of these countries to the empire of Prabhākara Vardhana. We also know from Bāṇa how two of these subdued countries rebelled in his last days, and had to be subdued again by his successor, Rājya. These were the country of the Hūṇas, and Malwa. But it is not clear from the evidence whether these countries were annexed by Rājya and brought under his direct rule. Next as regards the state of things under Harṣa, Yuan

[1] A most luminous exposition of what he calls the Doctrine of Maṇḍala appears in B. K. Sarkar's *Political Institutions and Theories of the Hindus*, Leipzig, 1922.

Chwang is our chief source of light. According to him, Gandhāra, which was overawed by the might of Prabhākara Vardhana, was now a dependency of the state of Kapis (Kāfiristan), to which were also subject 'more than ten of the neighbouring lands' [Watters, i. 123], among which are named Lampa (Laghman), Nagar (Jelalabad), and Fa-la-na (in the Kurum river district). Like Kapis, Kashmir was also a similar large state owning a number of dependencies, viz. Siṁhapura, Uras, Taxila, Rājapura, and Punach (Pan-nu-tso). The third large state in the North was Che-ka (with its city of Sākala), with its dependencies of Multan and Po-fa-to (Parvata). Perhaps from the manner of Yuan Chwang's statements we have to infer that these states were outside the limits of Harṣa's dominion, but in two of these states, Kapis and Kashmir, the kings were at least Harṣa's brethren in faith. The King of Kapis, like Harṣa, held even the Mokṣa Pariṣad, 'at which he gave liberally to the needy', and had in his territories more than 100 Mahāyāna monasteries [Watters, i. 123]. Like Harṣa, too, he sought the company of Yuan Chwang, whom he escorted for some distance on his return journey [*ibid.*, ii. 269]. The King of Kashmir was also a devoted Buddhist, who, like Harṣa, had a high regard for the Chinese pilgrim who used to read and expound to him the Scriptures, and remained as his guest for two years for purposes of study. The king 'gave him 20 clerks to copy out manuscripts and 5 men to act as attendants' [*ibid.*, i. 259]. Yuan Chwang does not name the king, but, according to *Rājataraṅginī*, he should be Durlabha Vardhana, who ruled from A. D. 601–37. The *Life* tells of an episode narrated below which shows that Kashmir in a way acknowledged the suzerainty of Harṣa: the episode of Harṣa compelling the King of Kashmir to part with a relic of the Buddha. Bāṇa refers to the 'land of the Indus' as being subdued by Prabhākara and 'the inaccessible land of snowy mountains' subdued by Harṣa himself; and these phrases might signify Kashmir also, as has been already stated.

Yuan Chwang also mentions states in other parts of India which were ruled by different kings, and on that ground might be deemed as being independent of Harṣa's dominion. Thus Ujjain, Jajhoti (Chih-chi-to), and Maheśvarapura were each ruled by a Brahmin king; Pāryātra (Bairāt) had a Vaiśya, Southern Kosala a Buddhist, and Ku-che-lo (Gurjara) also a Buddhist king. If the last place was Gurjara, it is to be noted that, according to Bāṇa, King Prabhākara was a terror to these Gurjaras. Thus checked on the east by the empire of Harṣa, they tried to expand westwards. First they established a dynasty at Bharoch under Dadda I (A. D. 528), who was succeeded by Jayabhaṭa I and Dadda II, Harṣa's contemporary, who gave protection to a King of Valabhī against his attack. The second line of their expansion was towards the land of the Lāṭas, where they fully established themselves by the middle of the seventh century, as will appear from their Kaira grants of the years A.D. 629

and 639 [*IA*, xiii. 88, also the Sankheda Charter of A.D. 595 (*Ep. Ind.* ii. 19)]. The Lāṭas, as already pointed out, were previously subdued by Prabhākara. The expansion of the Gurjaras southwards was, however, checked by Pulakeśin II, whose suzerainty they accepted by about A.D. 634, as will appear from the Aihole inscription cited above.

Yuan Chwang mentions Sindh as being ruled by a Buddhist Śūdra king. On the other hand, Bāṇa tells us that Harṣa 'pounded a King of Sindh'. If we may believe in the *Chach-nāmā*, the Brahmin dynasty of Sindh founded by Chach and made famous by Dāhir was preceded by the dynasty whose last king was Sāhasi Rāi, whom it was accordingly that the Chinese pilgrim must have seen in about A.D. 641.

Matipur (near Hardwar) was also ruled by a non-Buddhist Śūdra king, and Suvarṇagotra (unidentified) by women; while in Eastern India, Monghyr was conquered by a neighbouring king and given over to the Buddhists, and Rājmahal (Kajaṅgala) 'had come under a neighbouring state'. But elsewhere Yuan Chwang states that 'King Śilāditya in his progress to East India held his court there', which probably indicates that this country was really subject to Harṣa after all.

Perhaps the only limitation of Harṣa's dominion in Bengal was furnished by the kingdom of Gauḍa or Karṇasuvarṇa under its anti-Buddhist king Śaśāṅka, the murderer of Harṣa's brother. It is not clear from the evidence whether Harṣa was able to punish him and subdue his kingdom, for, according to the inscription already cited, he was quite prosperous as a Mahārājādhirāja even in A. D. 619. Later on, however, as is shown in a note below, his kingdom had to surrender to the power of Harṣa's friend and ally, King Bhāskaravarman of Kāmarūpa. It may, however, be noted that Yuan Chwang, who had visited Karṇasuvarṇa some time between A. D. 636 and 639, does not mention the name of any king then ruling, from which we may infer with Mr. R. D. Banerji [*History of Bengal* in Bengali, 2nd ed., p. 109] that since by that time its old king Śaśāṅka was dead and gone, the province came to be a part of Harṣa's empire.

There is, again, evidence to show that Harṣa's dominion extended up to Orissa. The *Life* tells of his expedition to Koṅgoda or Ganjām, and his camping in Orissa, in the course of which he tried to do some propagandist work on behalf of his faith, Mahāyāna Buddhism, by arranging to hold there a religious conference, for which he sent for learned Buddhists from distant Nālandā, as related below. That Orissa was a province of his empire is apparent from the fact that he made an offer to assign to Jayasena, the most learned Buddhist of that part, 'the revenue of eighty large towns of Orissa', as stated in the *Life*.

Thus even if we exclude from Harṣa's empire the countries for which the Chinese pilgrim assigns other rulers, the territory of that empire was undoubtedly much larger than that of any other individual state of the times in Northern India. It comprised practically the whole of the United Provinces, a large part of Bihar and Bengal (with the exception of only Karṇasuvarṇa), Orissa, and such parts of the Panjab, Rajputana, Central and Western India, for which Yuan Chwang does not mention other rulers. The southern limit of his dominion must have been the river Rēvā or Narmadā on which was fought the great battle between him and Pulakeśin II. But as has been already stated, the Hindu political system did not favour much centralized control, but believed more in decentralization and local autonomy.[1] Thus the mere size of the territory directly governed by Harṣa would not be at all a correct measure of his true political position and achievements, the sphere of his influence. With all the possible reservations, it cannot be doubted that Harṣa achieved the proud position of being the paramount sovereign of the whole of Northern India. That the Indian public opinion[2] of the times held this view is clear from the description of Harṣa as 'the Lord of the whole Uttarāpatha' in even the South Indian inscriptions.

[1] The view taken here is also endorsed by Vincent Smith, according to whom 'the sway of Harṣa was undisputed over the whole of the basin of the Ganges (including Nepal) from the Himalaya to the Narmadā, besides Malwa, Gujarat, and Surāṣṭra. Detailed administration of course remained in the hands of the local Rājās, but even the king of distant Assam (Kāmarūpa) in the east obeyed the orders of the suzerain, whose son-in-law, the King of Valabhī in the extreme west, attended in the imperial train' [*Early History of India*, 3rd ed., p. 341].

[2] Bāṇa applies to Harṣa the following imperial titles, viz., Chakravartī, Lord of the field bounded by the five oceans, Parameśvara (85), Devadeva, and 'Sovereign of all continents' (100).

Yuan Chwang also records the same public opinion confirmed by his own observation when he says that 'Harṣa reduced the neighbouring states to subjection, invaded the states which had refused allegiance', and ultimately 'brought the five Indias (of Svarāṣtra, Kanyākubja, Gauḍa, Mithilā, and Orissa) under allegiance', and also that 'countries far and near were giving in allegiance to him' with the exception of Mahārāṣṭra, which 'refused to become subject to him', although Harṣa 'gathered troops from the five Indias and the best generals from all countries' against his enemy by his rights as suzerain.

We may measure, indeed, the extent and degree of his power and influence in Northern India by a few significant facts on record. His empire sometimes extended not by conquest or force, but by alliance and friendship. The king of distant Kāmarūpa (Assam) offered him allegiance of his own accord and was anointed king by his liege lord, as stated by Bāṇa (*atra devena abhiṣiktaḥ Kumāraḥ*). We read of another king of 'North India' or the Panjab, King Udito of Jālandhara, who became a convert to Buddhism; 'thereupon the king of "Mid-India" appreciating his sincere faith gave him sole control of matters relating to Buddhism in all India' [Watters, i. 297]. The king of 'Mid-India' was, of course, Harṣa, while the king of Jālandhara, according to the *Life* (p. 190), was also charged by Harṣa to conduct the Chinese pilgrim in safety to the frontiers, and placed himself in command of the mounted escort provided for the purpose. By virtue of his position as suzerain, Harṣa further commissioned four official guides to accompany the escort with letters written by the emperor (on fine white cotton stuff and sealed with red wax), which they were instructed to present in all the countries through which they conducted the pilgrim, 'to the end that the princes of these countries might provide carriages or modes of conveyance to escort the Master even to the borders of China' [*ibid.*]. The imperial wish, again, was complied with by the king of distant Kapis, who, as already narrated, had also escorted the Chinese pilgrim for some distance on his way home. Thus Harṣa's influence and fame extended all over Northern India and even up to the borders of China. Embassies were exchanged between him and the Chinese Emperor. A Brahmin envoy sent to the Chinese court in A.D. 641 returned in A.D. 643 with a Chinese mission bringing the reply. This mission, which returned to China in A.D. 645, was followed by another mission from China under Wang-hiuen-tse, sent with an escort of thirty horsemen [Smith's *Early History of India*, 3rd ed., p. 352].[1]

[1] We may also recall here in this connexion the inauguration of the Harṣa era as another proof of the superior political status achieved by Harṣa in his times. Kielhorn mentions twenty inscriptions as being assigned to the Harṣa era, of which Nos. 542 and 544 are now found to be connected with the Vikrama era. Of the rest, eleven inscriptions are in Nepal, one in Magadha, another in the Panjab, and the others in places near Kanauj. [See *Ep. Ind.* vol. v.]

There are also other accounts of the pomp and circumstance attaching to Harṣa's position as paramount sovereign. Bāṇabhaṭṭa describes[1] as an eye-witness how the royal camp pitched near Manitāra along the Ajiravatī river (on which stood Śrāvastī), 'was filled on every side with conquered hostile vassal chiefs' of whom 'some who could not find admission hung down their heads in shame', while others were permitted to present chowries or sword-blades in obsequious service to the emperor, and some others, 'honoured even in being conquered', were 'continually asking the servants of the different domestic porters who at intervals made their exits and entrances, and whose track was followed by thousands of various suppliants,—"Good sir, will it be to-day? Will the great lord give an audience in the hall after he has dined, or will he come out into the outer court?" and thus spending the day in the hope of an audience'. Besides the hostile chiefs, the emperor was attended by other kings 'who would come from the desire of seeing his glory'; 'natives of various countries who were waiting for the time when he would be visible'; 'Jains, Ārhatas, Pāśupatas, mendicants of the school

[1] This was Bāṇa's second visit to the emperor, the first visit being apparently not very successful. Early morning, after the performance of the due rites (gamana-maṅgala), he set out from his native place, Prītikūṭa. On the first day he crossed the Chaṇḍikā forest, and arrived at a village called Mahākūṭa, whence, next day, he crossed the river Bhāgīrathī, and rested for the night at a village. On the following day he reached Harṣa's camp. (See *HC.*)

of Parāśarya, Brāhmin students, natives of every land, and savages from every forest that fringes the ocean-shore, and ambassadors from every foreign country'. Bāṇa further informs us that the emperor's capital attracted as settlers even Āndhras and Dravidians from the far south (170). That the feudatories (Sāmantas) were a constant feature of the court of the emperor has been already seen: when Rājyavardhana marches against Malwa he asks Harṣa to stay behind with the feudatories; when Harṣa wanders about the Vindhya hills and forests in search of his sister, he is accompanied by Mādhavagupta, the prince of Malwa, and a troop of tributary kings. It was an Āṭavika Sāmanta or forest chief, again, who assisted Harṣa in his search for his sister in the Vindhyan forests. We have already seen how these Sāmanta kings, forming the nobility of the imperial court and bringing dignity to it, were always in attendance even with their wives on ceremonial occasions such as birth or marriage in the royal household. We shall also see later how some of the highest administrative offices of the empire were offered to these Sāmantas. We are further told by the Chinese pilgrim, an eye-witness of the events, that in the royal progress from Kajughira (modern Kānkjol, i.e. Rājmahal, according to Cunningham) to Kanyākubja, the emperor was accompanied by Kumārarāja, king of Assam, with his full retinue from his kingdom [comprising 20,000 elephants and 30,000 ships (*Life*, p. 172)], while at the actual assembly at Kanauj 'there were present kings of eighteen[1] countries of the five Indies' [*Life*, p. 177]. The same eighteen kings also followed in the suite of the emperor in his journey from Kanauj to Prayāga for purposes of his sixth quinquennial assembly at the confluence of the Gaṅgā and Yamunā. We are further told [*Life*, p. 185] that while the emperor pitched his tent on the north bank of the Ganges, his two favourite vassal-chiefs, Dhruvabhaṭṭa, 'king of South India' (Valabhī), and Kumāra-rāja of Kāmarūpa, located themselves respectively on the west of the confluence and the south side of the Yamunā. 'On the morrow morning the military followers of Śīlāditya-rāja and of Kumāra-rāja embarked in ships and the attendants of Dhruvabhaṭṭa-rāja mounted their elephants, and so, arranged in an imposing order, they proceeded to the place of the appointed assembly. The kings of the eighteen countries joined the cortège according to arrangement' [*Life*, p. 186]. It is further stated [*ibid.*, p. 173] that as the emperor marched, he was accompanied by several hundred persons with golden drums, who beat one stroke for every step taken by him—a form of honour reserved only for him and not to be adopted by other kings.

But the pomp and power of the emperor were indicated not merely by his command of the tributary chiefs, but also by his army, by which he could overawe the whole of Northern India. The distant king

[1] The *Si-yu-ki* makes the number twenty, which probably counted, besides the eighteen kings, the kings of Assam and Valabhī.

of Assam, when Harṣa sent for the Chinese pilgrim detained by him, at first thought of defying him, saying that the king could have his head but not his guest. 'I trouble you for the head,' came the prompt reply of Harṣa, whereupon Kumāra became submissive. A single word of the emperor was sufficient for the discipline of his subordinate chiefs. It was the army which made his power thus felt in the remotest parts of his empire. He commenced his conquests, as we have seen, with the initial army of 50,000 infantry, 2,000 horse, and 5,000 elephants [Beal, i. 213], by which he won the empire, and he maintained it by the increased force of 60,000 war elephants and 100,000 cavalry. Bāṇa has given some interesting details about this imperial army. The elephants which made up its main element and strength were 'acquired as tribute or as presents' by the emperor, or sent at the time of an embassy, or by the lord of a wild settlement. Some of them also came from 'the rangers of the elephants' districts'. They were, in the words of Bāṇa, 'collected to conquer all continents like so many mountains to make a bridge over the ocean' (65). The emperor's 'favourite elephant, his friend in battle and sport,' was named Darpaśāta, who 'seemed to pour out again from his mouth the river which he had drunk up in his triumphal progress of conquest' (75). He had a strong contingent of horses. The royal stable was supplied with horses from different countries, 'from Vanāyu, Āraṭṭa, Kamboja, Bharadvāja, Sindh, and Persia' (70). They were guarded by the Chaṇḍālas, while 'the tutelary deity (Govinda) was worshipped before them' (72). The staff for elephants and horses included, as mentioned by Bāṇa, (1) the *Kaṭuka*, elephant rider; (2) *Nālivāhika*, elephant groom or fodderer; (3) *Vallabhapāla* or *Aśvapāla*, marshal or groom; (4) *Anāyatta*, groom; (5) *Hastipārśvarakṣī*, groom; and (6) *Ghāsikā*, fodderer. Elephant manœuvres were organized, and called *Karikarma*. Bāṇa gives the further interesting information that the imperial army had also included troops of camels (66). The inscriptions always refer to 'the victorious camp of Harṣa as being furnished with boats, elephants, and horses'.[1]

[1] In connexion with the extent of Harṣa's empire, it may be noted that an old Kanarese Inscription has been recently found in the Shimoga District of Mysore, which states that 'while Sila-āditya, the light of the quarters, the most powerful, and a thorn in the way of the bravest, ascended the throne of the empire', his general, Pettaṇi Satyāṅka, fell fighting in battle against the army of Mahendra. Dr. R. Shama Sastri, the Director of Archaeology in Mysore, considers [Mysore Arch. Rep for 1923, pp. 8, 83] that this 'Sila-āditya' might be no other than Śilāditya Harṣa, whose suzerainty had probably thus extended as far south as Shimoga against Mahendra, who might be identified with his contemporary Pallava king, Mahendravarman I. It is, however, not easy to understand how Harṣa could possibly have established any connexion with the far south, when its very beginnings were so effectively checked on the northern frontiers of the Deccan by his great adversary, Pula Keśin, as narrated in the text.

NOTES

A. *On some of the Contemporaries of Harṣa.*

THERE are three names associated with the history of Harṣa, of which the proper identification is still a subject of controversy. These names are Devagupta, King of Malwa, who, according to an inscription cited in the text, was defeated and killed in battle by King Rājyavardhana; and Kumāragupta and Mādhavagupta, the two princes of Malwa, who figure in the *Harṣa-charita* not as foes, but as the friends and companions of both Rājya and Harṣa as princes. Kumāragupta is not subsequently heard of, but Mādhavagupta, in Bāṇa's account, accompanies Harṣa, along with other tributary kings, in his wanderings in search of his sister, even after the defeat inflicted upon Malwa by Harṣa's brother. We are, therefore, called upon to explain how a prince of Malwa was living at the court of Harṣa as his friend, while another prince was cultivating a different relationship, and brought upon him the vengeance of the house of Harṣa by his aggressions against the allied house of the Maukharis of Kanauj. We can only explain this apparent anomaly by tracing the historical relations between all the three powers concerned, viz. the Guptas of Malwa, the Maukharis of Kanauj, and the Vardhanas of Thāneṣar. The sources of their history are about ten inscriptions, besides some coins of a few apparently Maukhari kings, of which the precise significance still remains to be settled. The inscriptions are described in Fleet's *Gupta Inscriptions* (vol. iii of *Corpus*) as follows:—

1. Aphsad Stone Inscription of Ādityasena (No. 42).
2. Shāhpur Stone Image Inscription of Ādityasena (No. 43).
3. Mandār Hill Inscription of Ādityasena (Nos. 44 and 45).
4. Deo-Baraṇārk Inscription of Jīvitagupta II (No. 46).
5. Aśīrgadh Copper Seal Inscription of Śarvavarman (No. 47).
6. Barābar Hill Cave Inscription of Anantavarman (No. 48).
7. Ṅāgārjunī Hill Cave Inscription of Anantavarman (Nos. 49 and 50).
8. Jaunpur Stone Inscription of Īśvaravarman (No. 51).
9. Sonpat Copper Seal Inscription of Harṣavardhana (No. 52).
10. Harāhā Inscription of the reign of Īśānavarman (studied in *Ep. Ind.*, vol. xiv). Nos. 1, 4, 5, and 10 help us to fix the chronology of the Gupta and Maukhari kings as follows:—

Guptas.

1. Kṛiṣṇagupta[1]
2. Harṣagupta
3. Jīvitagupta I
4. Kumāragupta III
5. Dāmodaragupta
6. Mahāsenagupta
7. Mādhavagupta
8. Ādityasena
9. Devagupta
10. Viṣṇugupta
11. Jīvitagupta II

Maukharis.

1. Harivarman
2. Ādityavarman *m.* Harṣā, sister of Harṣagupta
3. Īśvaravarman
4. Īśānavarman
5. Śarvavarman[2]
6. Susthitavarman
7. Avantivarman
8. Grahavarman (mentioned by Bāṇa but not in the inscriptions).

Of these kings, Nos. 1–8 of the Gupta list are mentioned in the Inscription No. 1, and Nos. 7–11 in No. 4; in

[1] Dr. Bloch infers from a clay seal found in Basarh, which mentions Govindagupta as a son of Emperor Chandragupta II by his wife Dhruvasvāminī, that Govindagupta was the same as this Kṛiṣṇagupta, the founder of this second Gupta dynasty. The imperial line of Chandragupta II was continued by his other son Kumāragupta I. But the probable date of Kṛiṣṇagupta does not tally with that of a son of Chandragupta II, as noted by Dr. Bloch himself [*A. S. R. Annual*, 1903–4].

[2] The Harāhā inscription mentions a brother of his, Sūryavarman by name, who might have predeceased his father or come after his brother and hence could not succeed to the throne.

the Maukhari list, No. 8 is not mentioned in any inscription, but in the *Harṣa-charita*.

It is to be noted that the inscriptions themselves say nothing as to the territories of these kings. But they tell us of the hereditary feuds between the Guptas and Maukharis, of which the last stage is related by Bāṇa when he tells us that the son of Avantivarman, Grahavarman Maukhari of Kanauj, was killed by a Gupta king of Malwa. The inscriptions do not mention Grahavarman, but they mention Avantivarman whom Bāṇa mentions as his father.[1] Thus Bāṇa helps us to locate the kings and understand their political relations.

Bāṇa states that it was a Gupta king, and a king of Malwa, who had murdered Grahavarman, but does not mention his name; but we know from the Madhuban Inscription that a Gupta king named Devagupta was defeated by Rājyavardhana, and so we take Devagupta to be the adversary of Grahavarman. Bāṇa names two princes of Malwa,[2] Kumāragupta[3] and Mādhavagupta, as being the companions of both Rājya and Harṣa, while Inscription No. 1 mentions a Mādhavagupta, and

[1] Bāṇa (223) refers to an ancestor of the Maukhari kings, Kṣatravarman by name, who in his foolish fondness for troubadours harboured some who were his enemy's emissaries and treacherously murdered him.

[2] This evidence of Bāṇa is very important as proving that the later Gupta kings, whose list is given on p. 52, are not to be regarded as the Gupta kings of *Magadha* but of *Malwa*, until we come to Mādhavagupta, as explained below. This view is against the received opinion of most scholars on the subject, although vague conjectures about a Gupta dynasty in Malwa are sometimes made by them [e.g. R. D. Banerji's *History of Bengal* in Bengali, 2nd ed., p. 105].

[3] Bāṇa also refers to a curious story (*vārtā*) that Harṣa rescued Śrī Kumāra of Malwa (probably this Kumāragupta) from the grasp of a mad elephant (100).

describes him as 'wishing for the company of Śrī Harṣa Deva' (i. e. Harṣa). Thus the statements of both Bāṇa and the inscriptions again get connected, and throw their combined light on the obscure history of these kings.

If, with Hoernle [*JRAS*, 1903], we identify Mādhavagupta, the friend of Harṣa, with the king No. 7 of the same name in the Malwa list, we must work out Malwa history as follows: Devagupta must have been the elder brother of Mādhavagupta (as well as Kumāragupta), and succeeded to the throne of Malwa after his father Mahāsenagupta. As King of Malwa, he followed in the footsteps of his predecessors in trying to extend his kingdom at the cost of his hereditary enemies, the Maukharis of Kanauj, who were then bidding for political supremacy in that region after the break-up of the Gupta Empire and the collapse of the Hūṇas after their defeat by Yaśodharman and Bālāditya. The imperial ambitions of the Maukharis were first embodied in Īśvaravarman, who, according to Inscription No. 8, extended his conquests towards the west up to Dhārā, to the Vindhya and Raivataka (Girnār) mountains in pursuit of the Andhras; also in Īśānavarman, who, according to Inscription No. 10, before he ascended the throne had achieved three important victories in three different regions, viz. victories over the Andhras,[1] the Śūlikas,[2]

[1] In Inscription No. 8 we find a reference to 'the lord of the Andhras wholly given over to fear, and taking up his abode in the crevices of the Vindhya mountains' at the expedition of Īśvaravarman. There is also a reference to the 'warrior of the Andhra army'.

[2] Probably connected with the country called *Śaulika* in the Bṛihatsaṁhitā [xiv. 8], and the Mārkaṇḍeya Purāṇa [lv], located in the south-east along with Kaliṅga, Vidarbha, Chedi, &c., as pointed out in the *Ep. Ind.* [xiv. 112]. The Śūlikas might be the Chālukyas. We know of a Chālukya king. Kīrtivarman I,

and the Gauḍas[1] of the sea-shore, and, according to Inscription No. 1, a fourth victory over the Malwa king, Kumāragupta. For these victories Īśānavarman won the title of Mahārājādhirāja, a title which was also deserved by his son Śarvavarman [who is called in Inscription No. 5 as Śarvavarman Maukhari, and in No. 1 only as Maukhari] by his victory over Dāmodaragupta of Malwa, who was killed in the battle. Malwa, however, avenged this insult by the victory achieved by her next king, Mahāsenagupta, over the Maukhari king Susthitavarman,[2] and the fame of the victory was sung as far as the banks of the Lohitya![3] But the fortunes of Malwa had a final set-back in the defeat of Devagupta by Rājya, followed by the annexation of that kingdom by Harṣa, as related by Bāṇa.

If this history is true, we have to suppose that the line of Gupta kings in Malwa came to an end with Devagupta, but continued under Mādhavagupta and his successors in another part of the country indicated by the localities of the inscriptions. No. 1 is from Aphsad in Gaya District,

extending his conquests up to Vaṅga, Aṅga, Magadha, &c. [Mahākūṭa Pillar Inscription].

[1] Are these the Gauḍas of whom Śaśāṅka, the invincible adversary of Harṣa, was the king a few generations later?

[2] Some historians identify this king with a king of Kāmarūpa of that name, on the ground that the river of Kāmarūpa, viz. Lauhitya (Brahmaputra), is mentioned here as the limit of Mahāsenagupta's conquests. But the content of the inscription rather shows that it is concerned more with the wars between the Guptas and the Maukharis than with their distant conquests, and so Susthitavarman may be a Maukhari. This view is also taken by Dr. F. W. Thomas (in his Introduction to the *Harṣa-charita* translation) and Fleet.

[3] This expression does not indicate that his actual conquests extended up to the Brahmaputra, or Assam, by the defeat of its king, Susthitavarman.

No. 2 from Bihar, No. 3 from Bhagalpur, and No. 4 from Arrah. It is also significant that No. 4 gives us only the genealogy of this new line of Gupta kings which starts from Mādhavagupta. Thus the facts seem to be that, after the annexation of Malwa, Harṣa provided for his friend, Mādhavagupta. by placing him in charge of some eastern parts of his Empire, and on the death of Harṣa this new kingdom rendered a good account of itself by reviving some of the lost glories of the Imperial Guptas of Magadha under the powerful successor of Mādhavagupta, viz. Ādityasenadeva, whose extensive conquests made him assume the imperial titles of Paramabhaṭṭāraka and Mahārājādhirāja and perform horse sacrifices in celebration of his imperial status. A strong ground supporting this version of the facts is supplied by the date 66 of Harṣa era, i. e. A. D. 672, given for Inscription No. 2 of Ādityasena. For this date will fit in with that of his father Mādhavagupta as the friend of Harṣa. On this view of the facts it is also clear that, as Ādityasena of Magadha had no direct connexion with Devagupta of Malwa, the name of the latter is not mentioned in the genealogy of the former[1] as given in Inscription No. 1. It is also significant that when Yuan Chwang visited Malwa or Ujjain, he saw there a Brahmin king who in that case must have replaced the Guptas whose line ended with Devagupta.

Regarding now the Maukharis, if we may take the localities of their inscriptions as indications of the extent of their power, it was the largest under Śarvavarman,

[1] The best precedent for such omissions is the Bhitarī Seal Inscription, which gives the genealogy of the Imperial Guptas from Gupta to Kumāragupta II without mentioning Skandagupta, because his line had ended with him and passed on to that of his brother Puragupta.

who is called in No. 1 as simply the *Maukhari* as the most distinguished scion of his house, and in Nos. 4 and 5 is described to have held sway from Arrah to Burhānpur, where the two inscriptions were found. The extent of this Maukhari expansion will be evident from the fact that originally they belonged perhaps to Aṅga or Bihar, as will be apparent from the Barābar and Nāgārjuni Hill Cave Inscriptions, Nos. 6 and 7, of Anantavarman described as the son of Śārdūla 'of Maukhari family', himself the son of Yajñavarman. Anantavarman achieved the status of a *Sāmantachūḍāmaṇi*, i. e. of a chief rather than that of a king. The newly achieved political dominance of the Maukhari house is also reflected in its coinage. There have been found coins[1] issued by some of their kings, viz. by Īśānavarman, on whose coins are read the figures 54, 55; Śarvavarman with the figures 58, 234 on his coins; and Avantivarman with his coins bearing the figures read as 67, 71, and 250. It is supposed that the figures in three digits stand for years of the Gupta era, in which case the dates of these kings would be between A. D. 553 and 569.[2] These dates will

[1] An important find of these coins is described by R. Burn, C.S I., I.C.S., in *JRAS*, 1906. It comprised nine coins of Īśānavarman, six of Śarvavarman, and seventeen of Avantivarman discovered for the first time. Besides coins, the Maukharis also issued seals, two of which were found in Nālandā along with Harṣa's seals. One of these shows a part of its original inscription, giving the Maukhari genealogy in which can be read the names of the founder Harivarmā, and of his wife Jayasvāminī. The inscription left on the other seal mentions 'King Īśānavarmā known for his knowledge of Varnāśramadharma and keeping his subjects contented (rañjitaprakṛiteh)'. On the top of both the seals appears the symbol of a well-moulded bull walking to left, with an attendant on either side [*Arch. Sur. Report*, Eastern Circle, 1917-18, p. 44].

[2] The year 611 of the Harāhā Inscription is taken to be a year in

fit in with the known date of Avantivarman's successor, Grahavarman, who was married to Harṣa's sister in the time of his father and was King of Kanauj before A.D. 606, when Harṣa became king. The numbers in two digits must point to years in some other era, and it has been suggested it might be a Maukhari era beginning from, say, A. D. 553–54 = A. D. 499,[1] the time of either Īśvaravarman or Īśānavarman, who started the era in imitation of the Imperial Guptas whom they succeeded to political supremacy by their conquests. The beginning of the Maukhari conquests was made by Īsvaravarman,[2] as will appear from his Inscription No. 51 from Jaunpur, which must have been already subject to his authority. The *Deo-Baraṇārk* Inscription of Jīvitagupta II (No. 4 on p. 51) also indicates that the authority of Śarvavarman and Avanti-

the Vikrama era and hence equivalent to A. D. 554, which is the same date for Īśānavarman as is given by his coins too. This is a remarkable coincidence of epigraphic with numismatic evidence on Maukhari chronology.

The date A. D. 553 for Īśānavarman leads us, however, to the position that both he and his successor were ruling and issuing coins in the same time. Cunningham even noticed a coin of Īśānavarman bearing the date 257 A. D. = 576. Thus there must be some error in the reading of the dates concerning Śarvavarman [see *Ep. Ind.*, xiv, 114]. N. G. Majumdar [*IA*, 1917, p. 126] recently found that the date-marks on Śarva's coins had 'totally disappeared'.

[1] The date of the composition of his great astronomical work by Āryabhaṭṭa, and of the expiry of 3,600 years of the Kaliyuga. This circumstance also makes the starting of a new era from A. D. 500 probable [*JRAS*, 1906, p. 848].

[2] As pointed out by N. G. Majumdar [*IA*, 1917, pp. 126–7], it is clear from the Harāhā Inscription that the extensive conquests of Īśānavarman were achieved during the reign of his father Iśvaravarman, who, accordingly, must be regarded as the first Maukhari to have attained an imperial status (see line 13 of the inscription).

varman extended as far as Arrah where the inscription was found, considering that the grant of Jīvitagupta II is stated to be not an original grant, but only a confirmation of that of the two Maukhari kings, and also of Bālāditya,[1] whom they had probably succeeded in power.

Besides the Guptas of Eastern Malwa and the Maukharis of Kanauj, Dr. Hoernle [*JRAS*, 1903, p. 545] introduces what he calls the Mālava Empire as the third factor to be considered in the then political situation of Northern India. The founder of this Malwa Empire was Janendra Yaśodharman Vikramāditya, originally a chief of the Mālava Clan, and a feudatory of the early Gupta Empire, who rose into prominence by his crushing victory over the Hūṇas before A. D. 533, by which date he delivered the Gupta Empire from barbarian tyranny. Thus he easily supplanted the then Gupta Emperor (who might be either Bhānugupta or Bālāditya), and in his Mandasor pillar inscription, he asserts that he not only conquered the Hūṇas but had won an empire larger than that of the Guptas, including, for instance, even Kashmir, as stated in the *Rājataraṅgiṇī* [ii. 7; iii. 125, with Stein's notes]. He had a long reign of fifty years from A. D. 533 to A.D. 583, and was succeeded by his son Śīlāditya, the King of

[1] This may be the same Bālāditya as is mentioned by Yuan Chwang to have defeated and taken prisoner, as King of Magadha, the Hūṇa king Mihirakula, which probably took place in about A. D. 525. This is fully explained below. There is, however, it may be noted, a point of serious doubt in the statement of Yuan Chwang when he says that this Mihirakula (A. D. 502-30) had lived 'centuries' before his time. This inaccuracy has led many scholars to cast aside the history as presented by Yuan Chwang on this particular point. What adds to the confusion about Bālāditya is that there are three Bālādityas known from the Gupta Inscription No. 79 of about A. D. 600, the first of whom is supposed by Fleet to have been the same by date as Yuan Chwang's Bālāditya.

Malwa, who, according to Yuan Chwang, had reigned sixty years before his visit, i. e. about 640–60 = A.D. 580. But Śīlāditya was not as powerful and successful a ruler as his famous father. The *Rājataraṅgiṇī* [iii. 330] tells us that he was dethroned by his enemies but afterwards replaced in the kingdom of his father by the King of Kashmir, Pravarasena II, a son of the infamous Toramāṇa [*RT.* iii. 104–9], and hence a Hunic king. Thus while Vikramāditya was the deliverer of his country from the Hūṇas, his son Śīlāditya was a supplicant for their protection!

Now, who were the enemies of Śīlāditya against whom he could not prevail and sought the aid of the Hūṇas? They were all the neighbouring kings who did not forget the usurpation of imperial authority by the upstart Yaśodharman, and had besides their own claims to it to assert. They were the Maukharis of Kanauj, the Vardhanas of Thānesar, and the Guptas of Eastern Malwa, an offshoot of the old Imperial Gupta House. Matrimonial alliances had further united them against their common enemies, the Empire of Mālava and the Hūṇas. The Gupta princess, Harṣā, as shown in Inscription No. 5, was married to the Maukhari king Ādityavarman, while another Gupta princess, Mahāsenaguptā, was married to Harṣa's grandfather, Ādityavardhana.[1]

[1] On the analogy of Harṣā and Mahāsenaguptā being the sisters of Harṣagupta and Mahāsenagupta, we may consider Bhānuguptā, mentioned in Inscription No. 35 of Fleet, to have been a sister of the Emperor Bhānugupta (c. A. D. 500) whose date will tally with *her* date. In the inscription the date of her grandson, Dakṣa, is given as A. D. 533, when he was minister. If we assume that Dakṣa was born in A. D. 513, his father must have been born in A. D. 495, and his father's mother, Bhānuguptā, married to his grandfather, Ravikīrti, in A. D. 494. At that time Bhānuguptā's royal brother Bhānugupta was not a king, but a prince under the

The leader of this combination against Śīlāditya was Harṣa's father, Prabhākaravardhana, who regarded himself as a special rival of Śīlāditya from the fact that his wife, Queen Yaśovatī, was the daughter of Yaśodharman Vikramāditya. Thus it was a contest between a son and a son-in-law for the Mālava imperial throne. The result of the contest is referred to by Bāṇa (101). Prabhākara was 'an axe to the creeper of Mālava's glory'. At the same time he had to punish the Hūṇas as the allies of Mālava, and came to be regarded 'as a lion to the Hūṇa deer'. The humiliation of Śīlāditya is further evident from the fact that he was compelled to surrender a son of his to Prabhākara: for Bāṇa tells us that 'Yaśovatī's brother (i.e. Emperor Śīlāditya) presented his son Bhaṇḍi, a boy of about eight years of age, to serve the young princes', i.e. Rājya and Harṣa. The name Bhaṇḍi itself is a Hunic rather than a Sanskrit name.

Now we can work out from Bāṇa the date of this first Mālava war, which ended in the dethronement of Śīlāditya. The surrender of Bhaṇḍi marking that event was made, as Bāṇa tells us, about the time of Rājyaśrī's birth, which took place in A.D. 593 according to our calculation (see Note B).

But these old enemies of Prabhākara, viz. Malwa and the Hūṇas, troubled him in his last days. He had to send Crown-prince Rājya to fight the Hūṇas in the north, while Śīlāditya, having regained his throne in about A.D. 604 with the help of the Hūṇa king, proceeded against his old enemies, the Maukhari and Thānesar kings, with what results we have already narrated. The

emperor Budhagupta (A.D. 477–500). It is possible that after all Budhagupta was the father of both Bhānugupta and his sister. This assumption does not at least violate their chronology as worked out here.

second Mālava war was brought to an end by King Rājya in the summer of A.D. 606. The friend and ally of Emperor Śīlāditya in this war must have been the king named Devagupta of Malwa in the inscription, who is twice referred to also by Bāṇa, once as 'a man named Gupta' (224), as implicated in the conspiracy to which Rājya fell a victim, and, secondly, as 'a noble called Gupta' (251). We have already examined the position of Devagupta in the list of Malwa kings.

Thus, according to Hoernle's theory, based mainly on the *Rājataraṅgiṇī*, the King of Malwa against whom fought Prabhākara, his son-in-law, the Maukhari Grahavarman, and his son Rājya, was not a Gupta king of eastern Malwa, but King Śīlāditya of Malwa proper, among whose allies figured Devagupta of eastern Malwa and Śaśāṅka, King of Gauḍa. The only fact, however, that does not readily reconcile itself to this theory is that the inscriptions dealt with above show a number of Gupta kings of Malwa who were on terms of hereditary hostility to the Maukhari kings of Kanauj, and do not name Śīlāditya at all in that connexion, while King Śīlāditya of Mo-la-po (Malwa), to whom Yuan Chwang refers, has been identified by S. Lévi as the Buddhist King of Valabhī, known as Śīlāditya I Dharmāditya. Thus the version of Malwa history, and particularly of the connexion between that history and the history of Harṣa as worked out by Hoernle, is not yet free from difficulties. The confusion may be cleared up to some extent by the table given on pp. 64–5, showing the chronological and other relations between the kings of the several houses figuring in that age.

The following points are to be considered in fixing the chronology of these kings:—

1. Nos. III, IV, *a*, 7, and (*h*) are contemporaries;

No. III defeated No. 7. From the known date of No. IV we count backwards towards the unknown.

2. Nos. II, 6, and (*f*) are contemporaries. No. 6, described as King of Malwa by Bāṇa, sent his sons to the court of No. II to be the companions of the latter's sons.

3. The date, A. D. 565, of the marriage of No. I is obtained by assuming that his son was king in his sixteenth year, A. D. 583.

4. No. 6 sent his sons to be the companions of Rājya and Harṣa, who were only fourteen and ten years of age respectively in A. D. 600. Thus No. 6 is taken to have ruled up to A. D. 600 at least.

5. Nos. II and (*g*) are contemporaries and relations, the former marrying his daughter, Rājyaśrī, to the son of the latter, No. (*h*). If Rājyaśrī was married at eight in accordance with orthodox ideals, No. (*g*) should have lived up to A. D. 600, Rājyaśrī being born in A. D. 593, as already shown.

6. The dates of Nos. (*d*), (*e*), (*f*), (*g*) are obtained from their coins or inscriptions already noticed.

7. The dates of Nos. 4, 5, 6 are obtained by their synchronism with (*d*), (*e*), (*f*).

8. Nos. 1–7 are to be taken as Gupta kings of eastern Malwa, as explained already.

9. No. *α* could have started as a king of Magadha only after the passing away from that region of the masterful personality of the Gauḍa king, Śaśāṅka, i. e., after A. D. 630.

10. No. *β* could have been an emperor of Magadha only after the passing away of Harṣa, i. e., after A. D. 650.

11. Inscription No. (46) of Fleet mentions as predecessors of No. *β* in the sovereignty of Magadha not only No. *α*, but also the Maukharis (*g*) and (*e*), as also Parameśvara, or emperor, Bālādityadeva, probably the Bālāditya of Yuan Chwang who defended his kingdom of Magadha

Mālava Emperors

Yaśodharman
(A. D. 533–83)
|
Śīlāditya
(A. D. 583–93 ; A. D. 604–5)

Imperial Gupta [1]

Kumāragupta I (A. D. 414)
|
Skandagupta (A. D. 455)
|
Puragupta (A. D. 467)
|
Narasiṁhagupta (A. D. 469)
|
Kumāragupta II (A. D. 473)
|
Budhagupta (c. A. D. 477–500)
|
Bhānugupta } (c. A. D. 500–28)
|
Bālāditya }

Later Gupta		*Maukhari*
1. **Kṛṣṇagupta**		(a) **Harivarman**
2. **Harṣagupta**	**Harṣaguptā** married to	(b) **Adityavarman**
3. **Jīvitagupta I** (A. D. 540)		(c) **Īśvaravarman**
4. **Kumāragupta III** (A. D. 550)	defeated by	(d) **Īśānavarman** (A. D. 550)
5. **Dāmodaragupta** (A. D. 575)	„	(e) **Śarvavarman** (A. D. 560)

Vardhana	*Late Gupta*		*Maukhari*
Mahāsenaguptā married to I. Ādityavardhana about A. D. 565	6. Mahāsenagupta (A. D. 600)	defeated	(*f*) Susthitavarman (A. D. 567)
II. Prabhākaravardhana m. daughter of Yaśodharman (A. D. 583–605)	*a*. Mādhavagupta (A. D. 630–50); 7. Devagupta (A. D. 600–5)	defeated and killed	(*g*) Avantivarman (A. D. 600)
III. Rājyavardhana (A. D. 605) } Friends of *a*	β. Ādityasena (A. D. 650–75)		(*h*) Grahavarman (A. D. 605)
IV. Harṣavardhana (A. D. 606–48) } Friends of *a*			

[1] This chronology was first suggested by Mr. Panna Lal, I.C.S., and has been since accepted on all hands. It was fixed mainly by considering the earliest and the latest date for each king, as given either in his inscription or on his coin known up to now.

against the Hūṇa Mihirakula, and made him prisoner about A. D. 525 and before A. D. 530, when he was finally crushed by Yaśodharman. Thus Bālāditya might be the same person as the Gupta emperor Bhānugupta, or his successor, the last of the Imperial Gupta Dynasty.

Its later history may be recalled in this connexion. The emperor Budhagupta (A. D. 477–500) exercised authority from Malwa to Magadha. His feudatory ruled between the Yamunā and Narmadā in A. D. 485 [No. 19 of Fleet]. His silver coins dated A. D. 496 were found in Benares. The Sarnath Stone Image Inscription of A. D. 476 refers to him as the paramount sovereign in those parts, while the Damodarpur first and second plate inscriptions of the probable date of A. D. 481 [*Ep. Ind.* xv. 135–6] point to his sovereignty over Puṇḍravardhana (North and parts of East Bengal). After him the Gupta sovereignty in Malwa was lost to the Hūṇas under Toramāna (A. D. 500–2) and his son Mihirakula[1] (A. D. 502–30), who ruled for at least fifteen years (No. 37 of Fleet). An attempt was made in A. D. 510 by Emperor Bhānugupta and his vassal chief, Goparāja, of Malwa, to recover the lost ground, but it probably failed [No. 20 of Fleet]. The Hūṇa supremacy in Malwa is attested by Nos. 36 and 37 of Fleet.

Thus the sovereignty of the Imperial Guptas over Malwa was finally lost. A successful stand against further extension of the Hūṇa power towards Magadha was made by Bālāditya, as related above.

The Hūṇa supremacy in Malwa was destroyed by the Mālava Janendra Yaśodharman by his victories recorded in the inscriptions numbered 33, 34, and 35 of Fleet,

[1] The date 502 for Mihirakula's accession we owe to Jaina sources cited by Pathak [*Bhandarkar Commemoration Volume*, p. 217].

and dated A.D. 533.[1] He ruled as Emperor of Mālava for fifty years, and was succeeded by his son Śīlāditya, as pointed out above.

Echoes of the imperial Gupta authority in Malwa come from inscriptions of some petty chiefs like the Parivrājaka Mahārājas Hastin and Saṁkṣobha of the years A.D. 518 and 528, in which the actual names of the then Gupta emperors are not given, but only a general reference to their rule[2] [*Ep. Ind.* viii. 284–7, and No. 25 of Fleet]. It is, however, clear that Yaśodharman did not become an emperor till after A.D. 528.

But we hear no longer of the Guptas in Malwa till we come to King Mahāsenagupta and his predecessors ruling in its eastern parts. This new dynasty of the Gupta kings of Malwa must have arisen under the suzerainty of Yaśodharman after A.D. 533. The first two kings, Kṛiṣṇagupta and Harṣa, had to establish their position against powerful foes. The *dṛiptārāti*, particularly proud foe, of the inscription (No. 42 of Fleet) might be even Yaśodharman himself. The third king, Jīvitagupta I, made his power felt as far as 'seaside shores' [*ibid.*], i.e. on the Gauḍas. The fifth copper-plate inscription of Damodarpur is dated 224 of Gupta era (not 214 as read usually), i.e. A.D. 543, and refers to the Gupta sovereignty

[1] No. 35 referring to his suzerainty is dated A.D. 533; hence his conquests were achieved earlier, about say A.D. 530.

[2] R. G. Basak [*Ep. Ind.* xv] holds that these inscriptions point to continuance of imperial Gupta authority in Central India up to the time of the Uchchakalpa Mahārāja Sarvanāth described as a Gupta vassal in A.D. 533. He also thinks that Bhānugupta was not defeated, though Goparāja was killed in the battle in A.D. 510, since there was a Gupta vassal in that very region even in A.D. 518 and 528; and that Gupta authority was finally extinguished not by the Hūṇas, but by Yaśodharman in Malwa, and in Surāṣṭra by the Maitraka Bhatārka.

over Puṇḍravardhana. The sovereign's name is not legible. but he might be either Jīvitagupta I or his successor Kumāragupta. An epigraphist actually reads the name as Kumāra [*Ep. Ind.* xvii. 193].

The Gauḍas, however, were left to be subdued by kings more powerful than the Guptas, viz. the Maukharis, who also arrested the eastward expansion of these Guptas of Malwa.

Eventually both the Guptas and the Maukharis were lost in the Empire of Harṣa.

The Gupta history in Magadha was, however, revived by Mādhavagupta, and especially by his illustrious son, Ādityasenadeva, who lived to perform the horse-sacrifice on achieving his imperial position. There are many gold coins found in different parts of Bengal which are described as imitation Gupta coins, and traced to these later Guptas of Magadha of whom this Ādityasenadeva was 'the first king'. These coins include some showing horse-sacrifice, and may be thus reasonably ascribed to the Gupta king who performed the horse-sacrifice after returning from the Chola country. According to the Deoghar Inscription [Fleet, p. 213], Ādityasena after his conquests built a temple costing three lacs of gold *ṭaṅkakas.* The word *ṭaṅkaka,* used for silver coins, is used here with reference to 'these light-weight gold coins current during the time of these Guptas of Magadha', which were then known by this name, as ingeniously suggested by Mr. N. K. Bhattasali [*JASB*, NS, xix. 1923, No. 6, pp. 57–64].

B. *On some dates in the history of Harṣa and his predecessors.*

THE *Harṣa-charita* contains some statements which Hoernle has cleverly utilized to arrive at some fairly precise dates in the history of Harṣa and his predecessors. It is to be understood that the expedition of Rājya against the Hūṇas, Prabhākara's illness and death, Rājya's accession to the throne and his death, all took place in the course of a year, A.D. 605–6. Now when Rājya was sent against the Hūṇas he was young enough to have shown but a 'faint growth' of his beard, as Bāṇa tells us (166). He might then be only twenty years old at the most, for before that he received, as a companion of his age, the Prince of Malwa, Kumāra by name, then a youth of eighteen. Between Rājya and Rājyaśrī was an interval of six years (115), while Harṣa was only about two years old (as explained in the text) when his sister was born. Thus we may calculate that Harṣa became king at sixteen, in A.D. 606, and was born in A.D. 590. Rājya in A.D. 586, and Rājyaśrī in A.D. 593. Thus their father could not have married Yaśovatī, daughter of Emperor Vikramāditya, later than A.D. 585, and as he had married soon after his accession to the throne, the latter event took place about A.D. 583, the date of the death of Emperor Vikramāditya and of the resulting confusion. Thus Prabhākara ruled between A.D. 583–606. He was engaged in a ten years' war against Mālava whose king Śīlāditya, defeated and dethroned, had to surrender to his enemy his son Bhaṇḍi, in A.D. 593, the year that Princess Rājyaśrī was born. Śīlāditya regained the throne of Mālava about A.D. 604, when he proceeded against his old enemies, and finally brought on the second Mālava war which ended fatally for himself and his dynasty in A.D. 606.

It may be noted that this chronology is also confirmed by other known dates of contemporary kings. The date of Īśānavarman, the Maukhari king, is shown by his coin to be A.D. 565, while a comparison of their genealogies shows him to be a contemporary of Prabhākara's father, Ādityavardhana.

C. *Saśāṅka* (A.D. 600–25?) *and Bhāskaravarman.*

BĀṆA calls Śaśāṅka King of Gauḍa,[1] and Yuan Chwang, King of Karṇasuvarṇa 'in recent times [Watters, ii. 115], a persecutor of Buddhism [*ibid.*, i. 343], who broke up the Buddhist monasteries between Kuśinagara and Vārāṇasī [*ibid.*, ii. 43], threw the stone at Pāṭaliputra showing

[1] The Gauḍas probably first appear as a political power in connexion with the conquests of Jīvitagupta I, as described in Inscription No. 42 of Fleet, where the king is represented as striking terror into the hearts of people on 'seaside shores'. We next hear of their subjugation by Īśānavarman in his Harāhā inscription of A.D. 554, in which he is described as keeping within their own limits the 'sea-faring' (*samudrāśrayān*) Gauḍas. The next landmark in Gauḍa history appears in four copper-plate inscriptions (considered by Mr. R. D. Banerji as spurious for their mixture of characters of different centuries) of Faridpur, which mention the names of three kings, Dharmāditya, Gopachandra, and Samāchāradeva, as kings of Gauḍa, and also of their local governors and Viṣayapatis appointed to a province in their kingdom called Vārakamaṇḍala [*JASB*, vii. 289–308; x. 425–37; *IA*, xxxix. 193–8]. Samāchāra is called a Mahārājādhirāja in the fourth plate, and his existence is further attested by two coins preserved in the Calcutta Museum, which show, in characters of about A.D. 500, legends read by Mr. N. K. Bhattasali as *Samāchāra* on the obverse, and *Narendravinata* on the reverse, and also the bull-symbol used later by Śaśāṅka [*JASB*, NS, xix. 1923, No. 6, p. 55]. Thus there can be hardly any doubt that Samāchāra was the predecessor of Śaśāṅka as a Gauḍa king.

the Buddha's footprints into the Ganges [*ibid.*, 92], cut down the Bodhi tree at Gayā, destroyed its roots down to the water and burned what remained [*ibid.*, 115], and tried to violate the Buddhist temple there by replacing the image of the Buddha by that of Śiva [*ibid.*, 116][1]. Thus, though a king of Karṇasuvarṇa, he made his power felt over a much larger area. He seems, however, to have begun as a mere chief, if he is to be identified with the 'Mahāsāmanta Śaśāṅkadeva' of an inscription [No. 78 of Fleet]. Soon he became powerful enough in A.D. 605 to enter, as we have seen, into a combination[2] with the Gupta king of eastern Malwa to overthrow the other rival combination of the two powers of Kanauj and Thanesar. Śaśāṅkamaṇḍala was to replace the Prabhākara or Maukhari-maṇḍala as the leading state! For a time his scheme was successful: Kanauj was seized, Rājya was murdered, and an advance against Thanesar was planned, till Harṣa, a more powerful adversary, appeared on the scene, and completely outrivalled him in the race for supremacy in northern India. Bāṇa tells us how Harṣa's *digvijaya* commenced with elaborate preparations for war against the Gauḍa king[2] stigmatized

[1] The cause of this combination might be blood-relationship, Śaśāṅka being himself perhaps a Gupta, the son or a nephew of King Mahāsenagupta. As we have already noted, a MS. of the *Harṣa-charita* calls him Narendragupta. In that case, the Gupta who is stated in the *Harṣa-charita* to have seized Kanauj might have been Śaśāṅka himself, and Rājyaśrī's escape from her prison might have been under his orders, as inferred by Messrs R. D. Banerji and R. Chanda [see R. D. Banerji's *History of Bengal* in Bengali, 2nd ed., p. 106].

[2] Mr. R. D. Banerji suggests that the offer of alliance to Harṣa at this stage from the distant King of Kāmarūpa was really due to the latter's hostility to the Gauḍa king, Śaśāṅka, a hostility which ultimately ended in the annexation of his kingdom of Karṇasuvarṇa by the Kāmarūpa king, Bhāskaravarman, as related below. He

as 'this vilest of Gauḍas', or 'the vile Gauḍa serpent'. But his narrative, following its own course, does not recount the results of those elaborate preparations. He, however, hints that Śaśāṅka was forced not only to abandon his project of conquering Harṣa's kingdom of Thanesar, but also to part with his new conquest of Kanauj, where we find Harṣa installed with his sister. Harṣa thus succeeded so far, but no farther, in his efforts to avenge himself upon the murderer of his brother. Śaśāṅka then transferred his ambitions in a different direction, towards the east, where he seems to have achieved an imperial status by A.D. 619, if he is to be identified with Śaśāṅka Mahārājadhirāja as mentioned in a Ganjam Plate Inscription of that year, recording a grant of one of his feudatories ruling on the east coast [*Ep. Ind.* vi. 143]. Thus if he was shining in full glory in his own sphere (aptly called Śaśāṅkamaṇḍala by Bāṇa) in A.D. 619, we must conclude that he had prevailed against the best efforts of Harṣa to crush him. On this view there was then a second blot on the escutcheon of Harṣa as a Digvijayī, the first being that cast by the Deccan overlord, Pulakeśin II.

The political importance of Śaśāṅka is also indicated by his coins and seals. A seal he had issued as a Mahāsāmanta was found at Rohtāsgaḍh in Bihar. He issued gold coins under the title of Śrī Śaśāṅka. The obverse of these coins shows Śiva reclining on his bull Nandi, and, behind him, the disc of the full moon signified by his very name of *Śaśāṅka.* Thus he was a follower of the Śakti cult, which explains his antipathy to Buddhism

further suggests that Śaśāṅka must have been defeated by this combination, and the result of this defeat was perhaps seen in those coins of Śaśāṅka which are debased with a large proportion of silver mixed up with gold.

and his iconoclastic tendencies. The reverse shows Lakṣmī seated facing on lotus, holding lotus in left hand, and above, on either side, elephant sprinkling water over her [Allan, *Gupta Coins*, p. 147].

Thus Śaśāṅka, as King of Karṇasuvarṇa, established a sphere of influence which seems to have extended right up to Ganjam. How long he thus ruled may be gathered from some statements of Yuan Chwang. He refers to Śaśāṅka as having already passed away in A.D. 637, when the Chinese pilgrim visited the Bodhi tree which was uprooted by Śaśāṅka, but was afterwards revived by the Maurya king, Pūrṇavarman, whom Śaśāṅka had predeceased, being unable to stand the reversal of his wicked deed!

After his death, we find Harṣa, in A.D. 643, launching a successful expedition against the Koṅgoda country on the east coast up to which, as we have seen, the suzerainty of Śaśāṅka extended. As a result of that expedition, Harṣa had his own dominion extended up to that limit, and was thus in a position to propose a gift of as many as eighty townships in Orissa to a local Buddhist divine, and to think of holding a conference in Orissa to propagate his own faith of Mahāyāna Buddhism. Thus we may conclude that it was only after Śaśāṅka's death that Harṣa was able to feed fat his ancient grudge against him. We have evidence also to show that Karṇasuvarṇa, after Harṣa, passed under the rule of his protégé, Bhāskaravarman, King of Kāmarūpa. In the confusion following the death of Harṣa, this worthy took the side of the Chinese invader, Wang-hiuen-tse, to overthrow the usurpation of Harṣa's minister, Arjuna, in A.D. 648–9. Next, his triumphant entry into the capital of Karṇasuvarṇa is celebrated in an inscription recording a grant made from his camp there [*Ep. Ind.* xii. 65] and describing him as the subduer of 'hundreds of kings'. It is interesting to note in passing that this inscription names as many as twelve kings of Kāmarūpa who were predecessors of Bhāskaravarman,[1] so that it carries back the history of Assam to the fourth century A.D., and of these twelve kings, the last five are the same as those mentioned by Bāṇa—a remarkable proof of the trustworthiness of his narrative!

[1] A seal was found at Nālandā of Bhāskaravarman which mentions the names of eight of these predecessors of his [*JBORS*, 1919, p 302; 1920, p. 151]. The seal of Bhāskara was found along with the seals of his patron, Harṣa.

CHAPTER III

ASSEMBLIES

WITH his suzerainty thus achieved, Harṣa was able to reign in unbroken peace for more than thirty years, as stated by the Chinese pilgrim. During these years he achieved triumphs of peace which were not less than his triumphs of war. Thus his reign, like that of Asoka, was practically devoid of any political events, so to speak, but quite eventful in point of religion and culture. One of this latter class of events was the convocation of a religious assembly at Kanauj for the purpose of giving publicity to the doctrines of Mahāyāna, as expounded by the Chinese pilgrim in the Śāstra composed by him, of which the contents and merits were known to the emperor at his very first meeting with the pilgrim at his camp in Bengal at Kajughira. From that place orders were sent throughout the different kingdoms that 'all the disciples of the various religious sects or schools, the Śramans, Brahmins, and heretics of the Five Indies, should assemble in the town of Kanyākubja to investigate the treatise of the Master of the Law from China'. The royal progress from the camp to Kanauj was marked by due pomp and magnificence. The king with his guest, the Chinese pilgrim, marched along the southern bank of the Gaṅgā, while his friend and ally, the King of Assam, who had come to him with his guest in response to the imperial summons, marched along the northern bank. The two kings, thus divided by the stream of the river, led the procession, followed by their gorgeous staff of soldiers, in boats and on elephants, sounding drums, blowing horns, and playing on flutes and harps, and by a crowd of several hundreds of thousand people, till they reached their destination in ninety days, to find there, already assembled for their reception, eighteen other kings, 3,000 Mahāyāna and Hīnayāna Buddhist monks, 3,000 Brahmins and Nirgranthas, and about 1,000 Buddhist scholars from the Nālandā monastery. Seating accommodation was provided beforehand for 2,000 persons in two thatched halls,[1] with a throne for the full-size figure of the Buddha in gold.

The state entry to the assembly was made from his travelling palace, improvised for the occasion, by Harṣa represented as the god Śakra, and Kumāra as the god Brahmā, taking in procession the statue of the Buddha on an elephant, with a canopy and an umbrella in their hands respectively,[2] followed by two elephants carrying jewels and flowers, another carrying the Chinese pilgrim and the chief officers of the king, and as many as 300[3] other elephants carrying

[1] A great *saṅghārāma* with a tower 100 feet high on its east side, according to the *Si-yu-ki* [Beal's *Records*, i. 218].

[2] According to the *Si-yu-ki* [*ibid.*] both Harṣa and Kumāra had an escort of 500 war-elephants.

[3] 100 elephants according to *Si-yu-ki* [*ibid.*].

the princes, great ministers, and chief priests of the different countries. When the procession reached its destination, the Buddha statue was first conducted to the hall and installed on the throne, followed by the king and Yuan Chwang presenting it with offerings; then in order were admitted the eighteen kings, 1,000 selected Bhikṣus, 500 selected Brahmins and heretics, and 200 of the great ministers from the different kingdoms, while the rest of the assembly were seated outside the gate of the hall. Then the king opened the conference by inviting the Chinese pilgrim to take his seat on a couch and be the president of the meeting.

Yuan Chwang began by extolling the doctrines of the Mahāyāna, and, appointing a subject for discussion, called upon *Ming-hien*, a monk of Nālandā, to discourse upon it. The subject was also announced on a placard hung outside the assembly hall, on which Yuan Chwang further announced that 'if there is any one who can find a single word in the proposition contrary to reason, or is able to entangle the argument, then, at the request of the opponent, I offer my head as a recompense'. Thus until night there was no one who came forward to say a word, when the emperor, well pleased at the event, adjourned the assembly and returned to his palace, while others returned to their appointed resting places. Next day they again escorted the image,[1] the king, and the

[1] According to the *Si-yu-ki* (*ibid.*) it was not the full-size image, as high as the king himself, installed in the assembly hall, but

others, as before. Thus had passed five days of the assembly when some followers of the Hīnayāna, seeing that the Chinese pilgrim had overturned their school, filled with spleen, plotted to take his life. Getting scent of this conspiracy, Harṣa forthwith issued a proclamation that 'if any one should hurt or touch the pilgrim he shall be at once beheaded, and whoever speaks against him shall have his tongue cut out, but that all others who would seek profit from his instruction need not fear this manifesto'. This had the effect of making the opponents disappear from the assembly, which went on smoothly for another eighteen days.[1]

The *Si-yu-ki* gives a somewhat different account of the assembly. According to it the assembly was convoked not for the exclusive discourse of Yuan Chwang, but for 'the different men of learning who discussed in elegant language on the most abstruse subjects' [*ibid.*, p. 219]. It does not also refer to any plot against the Chinese pilgrim, but against the emperor himself. It appears that on the last day of the assembly a fire broke out in the tower as well as in the pavilion over the gate of the hall. When it was extinguished by the king's intercession, as it was believed, Harṣa with the kings went up to the top of the tower to have a view of the scene, and when descending the steps he was suddenly attacked by

a shorter image of gold, three feet high, and thus more portable as the *utsavamūrti*.

[1] In the *Si-yu-ki* the session of the assembly comprised twenty-one days [*ibid.*] and not twenty-three, as stated here.

a heretic, knife in hand, whom, however, the emperor skilfully captured. The kings then demanded that the assassin should be instantly killed, but Harṣa forbade it, and got from the assassin the confession that he was engaged to kill him by heretics who felt insulted at his treatment of them at the assembly. Harṣa then straitly questioned the heretics, 500 Brahmans, summoned before him, who confessed to their setting fire to the tower by shooting burning arrows, expecting that in the resulting confusion they would be able to kill him; but this plan having miscarried, they hired the assassin to do it. Then the kings and the ministers demanded the extermination of the heretics, but Harṣa only punished the chief of them, and pardoned the rest, banishing the 500 Brahmins to the frontiers of India [*ibid.*, p. 221].

At the conclusion of this assembly the emperor offered to Yuan Chwang in recognition of his merits 10,000 pieces of gold, 30,000 pieces of silver, 100 garments of superior cotton, while the eighteen kings wanted to present him each with rare jewels. But all these costly presents the pilgrim in a true religious spirit declined to accept. Next the emperor, not minding his objections and protests, mounted him on an elephant and took him in a procession with the ministers of state to proclaim that he had established the standard of right doctrine, i.e., Mahāyāna, and overthrown all opposing doctrines.

The next important religious event of his reign was his institution of a quinquennial assembly for the distribution of royal charities, called the *Mokṣa*. At the conclusion of his special assembly at Kanauj, Harṣa found that it was time for him to hold the sixth session of the other assembly, for which the place fixed was Prayāga at the confluence of the Gaṅgā and Yamunā, where, according to tradition, 'it was more advantageous to give one mite in charity than a thousand in other places', whence the place was called the 'Arena of Charitable Offerings'. On Harṣa's invitation to Yuan Chwang to accompany him from Kanauj to Prayāga for the assembly there, the pilgrim, though homesick, could not but accept the invitation, saying that if His Majesty did not grudge his treasure for the good of others, how could he grudge a short delay in his homeward journey? Thus they came to Prayāga, attended by all the eighteen kings, to find there already assembled about half a million of people. The 'Arena of Charity' was the great sandy plain, about five miles in circuit on the west of the confluence, where even to this day is held the most important and most numerously attended religious Congress of India, the *Kumbha melā*. Invitation was issued 'through the Five Indies to the Śramans, heretics, Nirgranthas, the poor, the orphans, and the solitary (bereaved) to come to the Arena of Charity and receive the royal gifts'. A square enclosure was made with a bamboo hedge measuring 1,000 paces each side, with many scores of thatched buildings in the middle in which the valuable treasures like gold, silver, and pearls were deposited, while less valuable articles such as the silk and cotton garments, the gold and silver money, were placed in hundreds of other store-houses within the same enclosure. Outside were made places for partaking of food. There were also erected some hundred long buildings where a thousand people might sit down for rest.

In addition to this, the emperor had his tent pitched on the north bank of the Gaṅgā, the King of Valabhī on the west of the confluence, the King of Assam on the south side of the Yamunā, while to the west of the position of the Valabhī camp were gathered all the recipients of bounty.

The proceedings of the assembly were begun by a military procession of the retinues of the emperor, of Kumāra Rāja, embarked in ships, of Dhruvabhaṭṭa Rāja, mounted on elephants, together with the eighteen kings.[1]

The first day's programme comprised the installation of an image of Buddha in a thatched building in the arena, followed by a distribution of the costlier kinds of clothing and other articles. The second and the third days were given to the installation of the images of the sun (Āditya) and Śiva (Īśvara), followed by a distribution of charity only half in value of what was given in honour of the Buddha. On the fourth day the distribution of gifts was reserved for 10,000 selected Buddhists, each of whom received 100

[1] This shows that the total number of kings assembled was wenty, as stated in the *Si-yu-ki*.

pieces of gold, 1 pearl, 1 cotton garment, besides various drinks and meats, flowers and perfumes. The next twenty days were reserved for the gifts to the Brahmins, followed by gifts to the heretics during the next ten days. Another ten days were spent in gifts to the seekers of alms from distant countries, while the eighth distribution was to the poor, the orphans and the destitute, occupying a full month. 'By this time the accumulation of five years was exhausted. Except the horses, elephants, and military accoutrements, which were necessary for maintaining order and protecting the royal estate, nothing remained. Besides these the king freely gave away his gems and goods, his clothing and necklaces, earrings, bracelets, chaplets, neck-jewel, and bright head-jewel—all these he freely gave without stint. All being given away, he begged from his sister (Rājyaśrī) an ordinary second-hand garment, and, having put it on, he paid worship to the Buddhas of the ten regions,' rejoicing that all his accumulated wealth and treasure were thus bestowed 'in the field of religious merit'. Thus at these quinquennial assemblies Harṣa made a record in individual charity.

This assembly being over, the Chinese pilgrim was detained for another ten days, when both Harṣa and Kumāra Rāja offered him 'gold coins and every sort of valuable', but he accepted only the gift of a fur-lined coat from Kumāra as a protection against cold on the roads. Harṣa then saw him off for a long distance. The pilgrim's belongings (books and images) were carried on horseback under the military escort provided by a king of North India called Udhita, but the advance being slow, the emperor had at once a great elephant attached to the escort of Udhita-rāja, and, himself taking several hundred light horsemen, overtook the pilgrim along with his companions, Kumāra and Dhruvabhaṭṭa, so as to spend some more time with him and take a final leave.

Among the other known events of his reign may be mentioned his forcible appropriation of a tooth relic of the Buddha from Kashmir, where the congregation at first concealed it under the ground when the emperor came in person to that distant place to see and worship it. But the King of Kashmir fearing the exalted character of Harṣa had the relic unearthed, and Harṣa then carried it off by exercising force. Harṣa enshrined the relic in a vihāra in Kanauj [*Life*, p. 181].

CHAPTER IV

ADMINISTRATION.

THE predominance of these religious events in the reign of Harṣa is but a testimony to its efficiency in maintaining peace and order and abolishing all sources of political troubles. Unfortunately, not much evidence is available regarding the administrative system which could thus leave the country free for the pursuits of peace and religion. Its success was inevitably due very largely to the king himself, to his realization of, and capacity to carry out, the duties and responsibilities attaching to his position as the head of the administration in charge of an extensive empire, which was, moreover, won not by inheritance but by his own deliberately designed conquests. The first requisite for an administrator is that he must have an intimate knowledge of his charge. Probably no one in the empire could equal the emperor in his knowledge of its different and distant parts, gained by his constant movements through them in course of his hunting, military expeditions, administrative tours, religious pilgrimages, or other adventures. His geographical knowledge of the northern parts of his empire was acquired in his early life, when he followed his brother in the campaigns against the Hūṇas, and hunted among the forests and hills of that part, and also in connexion with his visit to Kashmir. Next, we find him wandering among the hills and jungles of the Vindhyas in search of his sister, followed by his campaigns against Malwa and Valabhī, and his misadventure further south on the banks of the Rēvā, where his aggressive advance was arrested by a sovereign of the south. The period of his personal campaigning was followed by one of religious progresses and administrative tours. Like Asoka, he believed in travelling as a necessity for the ruler as much as for his officials, so that he may have a first-hand knowledge of the conditions of the people committed to his care. 'If there was any irregularity in the manners of the people of the cities, he went amongst them,' observes the Chinese pilgrim [Beal, i. 215]. The inscriptions tell us of two places where Harṣa was camping out while on tour, viz. 'Vardhamāṇakoṭi', from which the Banskhera plate grant was issued by the emperor, and 'Kapitthikā' (same as Kapittha of Yuan Chwang, identified with Saṅkāśya near Kanauj), from which was issued the Madhuban plate grant. The Chinese pilgrim further tells us how at the time of his visit 'the emperor was visiting different parts of his empire' [Beal, i. 215]. He first met the emperor when he was in camp at a place called Kajughira in Bengal, already referred to. Here 'he held his court in his progress to East India' [Watters, ii. 183]. He came to that place directly from his attack on Koṅgoda (Ganjam) [*Life*, p. 172], after spending some time in Orissa [*ibid.*, p. 159].

While camping out in Orissa he was interviewed by the adherents of Hīnayāna, who showed him a work by a teacher of a South Indian king, Prajñāgupta by name, which challenged the doctrines of Mahāyāna. The king said they had not seen the best exponents of Mahāyāna, on which they suggested that he might call a conference to settle the matter. That very day the king sent a letter with a messenger to Śīlabhadra, the Abbot of Nālandā Vihāra, asking him to send four learned monks for purposes of the conference. Harṣa could not, however, tarry long in Orissa, and so sent another letter to Nālandā, stating: 'There is no immediate pressure for my former request: let them wait, and afterwards come here' [*Life*, p. 159]. While on tour the emperor was accommodated in what are called 'travelling palaces'. One such was improvised on the occasion of his stay at Kanauj for purposes of the assembly [*Life*, p. 177]. It is also called 'pavilion of travel' [*ibid.*, p. 173], such as that built for him at Kajughira. These structures were made of cut grass like huts [Watters, *ibid.*], or 'built of branches and boughs', and were burnt on the emperor's departure [Beal, ii. 193]. That he was moving in great state is evident from the description already cited of his camp at Maṇitāra along the Ajiravatī river,[1] as given by Bāṇa. The imperial camp there

[1] Peterson [*Kādambarī*, introduction, p. 53 n.] has also pointed out that 'at the time of Bāṇa's visit, Harṣa was already supreme ruler in the north of India, and does not appear to have any *fixed* capital' and that in the *Harṣa-charita* he is not represented, as he

was surrounded by 'many camps of the renowned subject-kings', with all their several retinues. It comprised four different courts. In the fourth court the emperor gave audience under a pavilion, seated on a throne of pearl-like stone, with his feet resting on a footstool of sapphire and ruby. The approaches to the camp were marked by equal pomp and magnificence. Here the royal gate was all dark with crowds of elephants; there the place seemed all in waves with the plunging horses as they leaped up to the sky in their restless energy; in another part it was tawny with troops of camels; in yet another it was all white with its masses of white umbrellas or waving with thousands of stirring chowries. The entrance to the royal camp was regulated by door-keepers, the chief of whom was Pāriyātra, the king's special favourite, 'whom one who pursues success should treat with suitable ceremony'. Inside the camp was a stable filled with the king's favourite horses, as well as the state elephant named Darpaśāta. The pomp of these 'travelling palaces' was also enhanced by that of the emperor's royal guests.[1] King Kumāra of Assam visited him at his camp in Bengal, with his followers on 20,000 elephants and in 30,000 ships, as we have already seen. Yuan Chwang makes the following general remarks on this royal

is by Yuan Chwang, as having his capital at Kanyākubja, although the Chinese pilgrim gives frequent accounts of his 'progresses'.

[1] Harṣa himself in his *Ratnāvalī* (Act iv) describes the King of Vatsa's camp as being marked by 'valued steeds, elephants of victory, and groups of feudatories' (*Kṣubhṛtāṁ gṛha*).

practice of travelling as an administrative duty: 'The king made visits of inspection throughout his dominions, not residing long at any place, but having temporary buildings erected for his residence at each place of sojourn, and he did not go abroad during the three months of the rain-season retreat' [Watters, i. 344]. Even while thus travelling viands were provided daily for 1,000 Buddhist monks and 500 Brahmins from the royal lodges [*ibid.*].

Thus the sovereign himself was one of the best travelled men in his empire, and we know of the following places at least at which he had camped out in his progresses through his dominions, viz. Rājmahal, Kanauj, Prayāga, Maṇitāra (Oudh), and Orissa, besides Kashmir, Valabhī, the Rēvā and Ganjām (Koṅgoda), visited by him as an invader. The range of his travels may be also inferred from the fact that he had information about the martial fame and exploits of the Chinese emperor Tai-Tsung, to which he referred in his conversation with Yuan Chwang. Such information he could only gather from his travelling in the far north, as pointed out by Watters [i. 351].

But the sovereign was also one of the most hard-working officials. 'The king's day', says the Chinese pilgrim, 'was divided into three periods, of which one was given up to affairs of government, and two were devoted to religious works. He was indefatigable, and the day was too short for him' [Watters, i. 344]. 'He forgot sleep and food in his devotion to good works' [*ibid.*].

How busy the emperor always was is graphically described by Bāṇa in connexion with his interview with His Majesty at the royal camp 'pitched near Maṇitāra along the Ajiravatī river'. The emperor 'used to give audience after eating', and so Bāṇa, 'having bathed and eaten his meal and rested, when only one watch of three hours remained of the day, and when the king had dined', proceeded leisurely to the royal gate conducted by Mekhalaka, the king's messenger. On the way he observed one by one 'the many camps of the renowned subject-kings', and 'conquered hostile vassal-chiefs'. It was difficult even for kings to obtain an interview with the emperor. Bāṇa saw some of them 'spending the day in the hope of an audience', and others from afar, who had come there from the desire of seeing his glory, simply waiting for the time when the emperor would be visible. 'The track of the servants of the domestic porters, who at intervals made their exits and their entrances, was followed by thousands of various suppliants anxiously asking when they could possibly have a sight of the emperor' (68). 'Following the path indicated by the door-keeper,' the eunuch Pāriyātra, Bāṇa had to 'pass through three courts crowded with subject-kings, and in the fourth he saw King Harṣa, in an open space in front of a pavilion, surrounded at a distance by his attendants in a line' and armed, with his special favourites, including a prince of Malwa, seated near him, and himself seated on a throne of stone, clear like pearl, resting the weight of his body on his arm, which was placed on the end of the seat, and sporting with his subject-kings (78), with his left foot 'playfully placed on a large costly footstool made of sapphires, girt round with a band of rubies' (81).

None of the authorities give a proper description of the royal palace. But its grandeur may be inferred from that of his travelling-palaces already described. Glimpses of the grandeur of the palace, and of the royal capital too, are, however, given in the *Harṣa-charita* here and there. We learn that the capital at Sthāṇvīśvara resounded with sounds of triumph, booming of drums, songs of troubadours and minstrels, and bustle of business (170). Its principal street was 'the bazaar street' (171). The palace had a street wall which was whitewashed (158). We read of its stairs (171), and the prince descending from the palace (179). It seems to have had four courts (171), which were large enough to become 'seas of elephants and horses' on festive occasions (158). We read of its 'mosaic floors of red lead' and decorations with the painting of auspicious scenes and modelling of clay figures of fishes, tortoises, crocodiles, coconuts, plantains, and betel trees. An indication of its luxury is given by the fact stated that its 'crocodile-mouthed conduits[1] conveying scented water filled a variety of pleasure-ponds' (158). Within the palace grounds might be seen 'lions in their cages', upon which Harṣa's mother loved to feast her eyes before he was

[1] The *Ratnāvalī* mentions fountains called *dhārāyantra*.

born; varieties of apes and orang-outangs (vanamānuṣāḥ), rare birds, and mermen with necks bound in golden fetters; 'musk deer scenting the space all round them with their perfume; female *chamara* deer used to running about the house; parrots, śārikās, and other birds enclosed in gold-painted bamboo cages, and chattering copious wit; partridges in cages of coral', which were some of the presents sent by the King of Assam to Harṣa to seek his favour (245). Harṣa's father, King Prabhākaravardhana, lay sick in his inner apartments called 'the White House', where numerous lackeys thronged the vestibule, a triple veil hid the salon, the inner door was closed, the panels were forbidden to creak, and closed windows kept out the draughts (171). In the Moon Chamber (the chamber above the *Dhavalagṛiha*) crouched the silent ministers of state, the screened balcony was occupied by the ladies, and the quadrangle by the servants (172). Queen Yaśovatī used to sleep in her 'chamber on the roof', the walls of which were decorated with 'painted figures of chowrie women' and the awning with other embroidered figures. Its furniture included a couch and jewelled mirrors (141).

The princes seem to have been given separate houses. We read of Harṣa as prince descending from the palace and going on foot to his own quarters (179).

The pomp and luxury in which Harṣa lived as emperor is indicated in the statement of Bāṇa (227) that he bathed in golden and silvern vessels, and included among his gifts to Brahmins 'vessels of precious stones, silver and gold in thousands, myriads also of cows having hoofs and horn tips adorned with creepers of gold-work'. Even while he was on the march he was not without his full provision of luxuries. 'The king's hired porters carried his golden footstools, water-pots, cups, spittoons and baths, proud of being in charge of the sovereign's property; there were also bearers of kitchen appurtenances with goats attached to thongs of pig-skin, a tangle of hanging sparrows and forequarters of venison, a collection of young rabbits, pot-herbs, and bamboo shoots, butter-milk pots protected by wet seals on one part of their mouths which were covered with white cloths, baskets containing a chaos of fire-trays, ovens, simmering pans, spits, copper saucepans and frying-pans', while villagers awaited the touring king with presents of curds, molasses, candied sugar, and flowers in baskets (237). His dress comprised a snow-white lower garment radiant with shot silk-threads, a bejewelled girdle, and a thin upper garment spangled with worked stars (80). He wore a necklace of pearls and other ornaments, which made him look 'like a jewel mountain with its outstretched wings of jewels spread on both sides'. He had, like Chandragupta Maurya, women attendants, a chowrie woman, and even the shampooing attendant (83). Valāhikā and Padmāvatī are mentioned among the shampooing attendants of King Prabhākāravardhana, who was attended in his illness by many nurses named Hāriṇī, Vaidehī, Līlāvatī, Dhavalākṣī, Kāntamatī, Āvantikā, &c. (177).

Queen Yaśovatī had also her own attendants, of whom the chief was Velā (181), and Suyātrā a favourite (142). At the time of her delivery she was attended by 'great physicians holding various herbs and stationed at proper places' (141).

The palace establishment included doorkeepers [the chief of whom was Pāriyātra (70)], domestic porters with their servants (68), chowrie-bearers, chamberlains, chefs under a head, bodyguard, and the like. The higher staff included physicians [of whom Suṣeṇa and Rasāyana are mentioned as treating Harṣa's father in his illness (171 and 178)], the king's advisers, the Purohita, Pandits [among whom Gambhīra is mentioned as the Brahmin attached to Prabhākaravardhana (161)], and the court-poets like Bāṇa and Haridatta, raised to eminence by Harṣa [*Ep. Ind.* i. 180].

For the transaction of state business, couriers (*dīrghādhvaga*) were employed who 'continually went and returned' [Beal, i. 215]. Bāṇa was sent for by the renowned courier Mekhalaka (59). A courier was dispatched on a female camel to his son-in-law by King Prabhākaravardhana (160). We also read of 'footmen being sent ahead to secure a relay of villagers to show the way to Harṣa', as he hurried from the Panjab to the capital at the news of his father's illness (170). The news itself was delivered to him by the courier Kuraṅgaka with a letter from the king to Harṣa (168). On arrival at the palace, and seeing the king seriously ill, Harṣa 'in hot haste dispatched express couriers and swift camel riders one after another to procure his brother's coming' (179). That communication by this method was pretty swift is shown from the fact that a messenger from Assam delivered a letter to Nālandā after two days [*Life*, p. 169]. Bāṇa also refers to the employment of spies, whom he calls *sarvagataḥ* (p. 40, Bombay ed.).

We do not have much information regarding the actual system of administration. Next to the sovereign ranked the chief Ministers of State, who probably constituted a *Mantri-Pariṣad* or council. During the reign of Rājyavardhana, Bhaṇḍi, his cousin, seems to have been the chief minister, for on his death it devolved upon him to call a meeting of the Council of Ministers to determine the succession. Addressing the assembled ministers, Bhaṇḍi said: 'The destiny of the nation is to be fixed to-day. The old king's son is dead: the brother of the prince, however, is humane and affectionate, and his disposition, heaven-conferred, is dutiful and obedient. Because he is strongly attached to his family, the people will trust in him. I propose that he assume the royal authority: let each one give his opinion on this matter, whatever he thinks.' They were all agreed on this point, and acknowledged his conspicuous qualities. On this the chief ministers and the magistrates approached Harṣa and entreated him to assume the royal authority. This account is also given by Yuan Chwang [Beal, i. 211], and it shows that the Council of Ministers wielded real power in the state when the election of the king was in their hands.[1] Another evidence of the power of the ministers is shown by the fact that they seem to have been responsible for the mistaken policy which unfortunately led to the death of Rājyavardhana. 'Owing to the fault of his ministers he was led to subject his person to the hand of his enemy' [*ibid.*]. This implies that his ministers decided that Rājyavardhana should respond to the invitation of King Śaśāṅka to attend the conference where he was treacherously murdered. Yuan Chwang goes so far as to assert that 'a commission of officers hold the land' [Beal, i. 210].

That Bhaṇḍi was the chief minister of Rājyavardhana is also evident from the fact that he alone was directed to accompany Rājyavardhana in his expedition against Malwa with a force of 10,000 horse, and returned with the whole force of the King of Malwa, captured by Rājyavardhana in his campaign, 'with soiled garb and breast filled with the points of enemies' arrows' (223). Bāṇa mentions Avanti as Harṣa's 'supreme minister of war and peace' through whom the emperor issued his proclamations (218).

[1] That kingship in these days was not hereditary is shown from several cases. The emperor, Samudragupta, was chosen by his father to succeed him to the throne to the distress of 'others of equal birth', with the consent also of the king's council (*sabhā*), as stated in an inscription. Similarly, his successor was also chosen (*tat-parigṛhītena*) by Samudragupta. The king's council is called *Pariṣat* in No. 10 of Fleet [Bilsad Stone Pillar Inscription of Kumāragupta].

There are also mentioned a few other chief officers of the state. Siṁhanāda was Harṣa's Senāpati, or commander-in-chief, a friend of his father, foremost in every fight though far advanced in years. Harṣa treated him with great respect as befitted his father's friend, and it was by the dust of his feet that he took the vow of vengeance against the King of Gauḍa, teaching a lesson to all other insolent kings (212). Kuntala was the chief officer of cavalry, a great noble high in his brother's favour (209). Skandagupta was Harṣa's commandant of elephant force (220), probably the same officer as is mentioned in the inscriptions, where he figures as the *Dūtaka*, charged with the conveyance of the imperial grants, and described as 'Mahāpramātāra Mahāsāmanta the illustrious Skandagupta'. The inscriptions also name 'the keepers of records', Sāmanta Mahārāja Īśvaragupta (in the Madhuban Plate) and Bhāna or Bhānu (in the Banskhera Plate, *Ep. Ind.* iv. 211). The names of the engravers are also given, viz. Gurjara and Īśvara. Lastly, these commands of the emperor are spoken of as being issued to officers of different ranks and grades, such as 'the *Mahāsāmantas, Mahārājās, Daussādhasādhanikas* (not explained), *Pramātāras* (explained as "spiritual councillors"), *Rājasthānīyas, Kumārāmātyas, Uparikas, Viṣayapatis*, and regular and irregular soldiers (*bhaṭachāṭa*)'. The status of some of these officers points to the dignity of Harṣa's position as the paramount sovereign surrounded by officers who were themselves chiefs and kings.

Yuan Chwang tells us that both the ministers of state and the common officials received their salaries not in cash but in grants of land, being maintained by the cities assigned to them. The emperor set apart a fourth of the crown lands 'for the endowment of great public servants', and another fourth part for 'the expenses of government and state worship' [Watters, i. 176]. We are further told [*ibid.*] that those who are employed in the government service are paid according to their work'. 'When the public works require it, labour is exacted but paid for. The people were not subject to forced labour' [Beal, i. 87].

While payment in kind was the rule for the Civil Service, payment in cash was resorted to for military service. The soldiers were levied according to the requirements of service. Rewards were proclaimed after the issue of summons, and then the recruits were enrolled. The military were used to guard the frontiers, to punish the refractory, and mount guard at night round the palace [Beal, i. 87].

The standing army forming the National Guard was recruited from the heroes of choice valour with whom the military profession had become hereditary. Thus they could easily become experts in the arts of war. These hereditary soldiers were garrisoned round the palace to guard it in peace, and were called out to form the intrepid vanguard of the army in war.

Yuan Chwang saw the Indian army being still composed of the four traditional elements. The Commander-in-Chief rode on the war-elephant covered with coat of mail with sharp barbs attached to his tusks. He had a soldier on each side to manage his elephant. A leader was also carried in a chariot drawn by four horses and guarded by the infantry on both sides. The cavalry spread themselves in front to resist the attack and were very useful in carrying orders hither and thither. The infantry for their quick movements were best at defence. They were the pick of the brave. They carried a long spear and a large shield, and some a sword or sabre to dash to the front of the advancing line of battle. With their hereditary skill they were perfect experts in the use of all the implements of war. These are enumerated as spears, shields, bows, arrows, swords, sabres, battle-axes, lances, halberds, long javelins, and various kinds of slings [Beal, i. 83; Watters, i. 171].

With all his military strength (represented by a standing army of 60,000 elephants and 100,000 horse) and administrative measures, the emperor could not give an equal protection to all parts of his extensive dominion. His government in this respect compares unfavourably with that of the imperial Guptas. During their time the Chinese pilgrim, Fa-hien, travelled through India in perfect safety without even for once being stripped by brigands (A. D. 405–11), but a similar felicity was not the portion of his successor, Yuan Chwang, during the régime of Harṣa. Once in the Panjab after crossing the Chandrabhāgā (Chenab) and leaving the city of Śākala he had to pass through a palāsa wood where a band of fifty robbers fell upon him, stripped him of all his clothes and goods, and pursued him sword in hand till a Brahmin ploughing the field rescued him by raising an alarm by blowing the conch and beating the drum, which brought together eighty men with arms [*Life*, p. 73]. At another time, not very far from the metropolis of Harṣa's empire, leaving Ayodhyā, the pilgrim with eighty fellow-passengers on board a vessel was sailing down the Ganges when ten pirate boats, taking his ship in tow, brought it to the bank. Then the pirates, struck by Yuan Chwang's appearance, seized upon him as the best human sacrifice for their deity Durgā, bound him to the altar, and were sharpening their knives and the pilgrim was saying his last prayer, when a terrible typhoon arose which frightened the brigands as indicating the wrath of the gods and they set him free and remained to be his disciples [*ibid.*, pp. 87 f.]. On his return journey, the emperor had a military escort provided for his safety under a king of North India as has been already stated, but we are told that the country between Siṁhapura (Ketās) and Taxila was 'frequented by robbers', and the pilgrim and his party were in constant fear of being spoiled on the way [*ibid.*, p. 191]. The comparative insecurity of the times is also hinted at by Bāṇa, who tells us of villagers who, 'despondent at the plunder of their ripe grain and bemoaning their estates, censured the sovereign, as he passed along, at the risk of their lives, saying, "Where's the King? What right has he to be King?"'

(238); and also of complaints against the tax-collectors (*bhogapati*) and policemen (*chāṭa*) [*HC*, p. 286].

These stray cases of violence were not, however, indicative of the normal spirit of the people at large. Yuan Chwang himself admits that 'as the government is honestly administered, and the people live together on good terms, the criminal class is small'. He thus estimates the character of the Indians: 'They are of hasty and irresolute temperaments but of pure moral principles. They will not take anything wrongfully and they yield more than fairness requires. They fear the retribution of sins in other lives, and make light of what conduct produces in this life. They do not practise deceit and they keep their sworn obligations.'

Among such a peace-loving, law-abiding, and moral people, criminal administration did not present much difficulty. The violations of law were not very usual. We hear, however, of plots against kings. There was a plot against Harṣa himself, to which a reference has been already made. Treason was punished by imprisonment for life, and not by any corporal punishment. 'For offences against social morality, and disloyal and unfilial conduct, the punishment is either mutilation of limbs or deportation of the offender to another country or into the wilderness. Other offences can be atoned for by a money payment.' Trial by ordeal was also in force [Watters, i. 171–2]. Bāṇa (143) mentions the custom of jail-deliveries marking auspicious occasions. Thus Harṣa's birth freed the prisoners. According to Bāṇa (86), justice was in the hands of the *Mīmāṁsakas*.

In spite of this severity of the Penal Code, the government, according to Yuan Chwang, was 'generous', i. e., conducted on benign principles. It did not make any large demands either upon the liberties or the pockets of the people: 'Official requirements are few.' 'Families are not registered and individuals are not subject to forced labour contributions. Taxation being very light, and forced service being sparingly used, every one keeps to his hereditary occupation and attends to his patrimony.' This probably means that the people were comparatively left free from the interference and control of the central authorities characteristic of unitary states and their systems of over-government at the expense of local liberty and self-rule.

As the central government left the people to govern themselves as far as possible, it rested on very light taxation and was satisfied with a small amount of revenue. The main source of revenue mentioned is that derived from the crown lands, which amounted to a sixth of the crop according to the traditional standard [cf. Manu vii. 130, 131; viii. 308]. Revenue was also derived from trade: 'light duties were levied at ferries and barrier stations' [*ibid.*, 176]. We have no information as regards other sources of revenue except some from the inscriptions. The Madhuban Plate shows that the king's dues from a village comprised the *tulya-meya*, i. e., taxes depending on the weight and measure of the things sold, and *bhāga bhoga-kara-hiraṇyādi*, i. e., the share of the produce, payments in cash, and other kinds of income.

The generosity of Harṣa's government is proved by its expenditure as much as by its light taxation. 'Of the royal land (the main sources of the sovereign's income) there is a fourfold division: one part is for the expenses of government and state worship, one for the endowment of great public servants, one to reward high intellectual eminence, and one for gifts to various sects' [*ibid.*].

The enlightened character of the administration is also shown in its maintenance of a separate Department of Records and Archives. Both good and bad were faithfully recorded in 'the official annals and state-papers', and 'instances of public calamity and good fortune are set forth in detail' [*ibid.*, 154].

Some glimpses of rural government we get from the *Harṣa-charita*. While the emperor was passing through a village, 'the village notary (*akṣapuṭalika*, i. e, one in charge of documents) appeared with his whole retinue of clerks (*Karaṇi*) and said: "Let His Majesty, whose edicts are never void, even now bestow upon us his commands for the day".' Then he 'presented a new-made golden seal with a bull for its emblem' (probably symbolical of the Saiva worship of the imperial house) on which the royal decree might be inscribed (227). It may be noted that the expression *Mahākṣapaṭalādhikareṇādhikṛita*, 'one appointed to the post of notary-in-chief', occurs in the inscription of Harṣa too.

So far about the administrative system of Harṣa as can be known from the records of his own life and times. But we may usefully supplement and extend our knowledge of it from the records of the age, the entire body of the inscriptions of the Gupta kings and their successors, which reveal movements of thought and life, processes and institutions that continued up to, and even beyond, the time of Harṣa. These inscriptions are well worth study in this connexion, as helping us to a more concrete and complete view of the administrative system under which, as agreed by all historians,[1] India had seen some of her best days for a period of wellnigh four centuries, the spacious times beginning with the Gupta emperors and ending with Harṣa.

The emperor, the king of kings, is given in the inscriptions the titles of *Paramabhaṭṭāraka Mahārājādhirāja* [applied to Harṣa in his inscriptions], to which are added the titles of *Parameśvara* (as in No. 46 of Fleet's *Gupta Inscriptions*), *Samrāṭ*, (No. 33, *ibid.*), *Ekādhirāj* (No. 32) or *Paramadaivata* [in the Damodarpur copper plate inscriptions of Kumāragupta I, *Ep. Ind.* xv, 113], or *Chakravartin*[2] (No. 39 of Fleet).

The emperor is the centre of a group of subordinate kings who belong to his system and move round him

[1] According to Vincent Smith, for instance, 'India was never governed better after the Oriental manner than under Chandragupta II'.

[2] In the *Ratnāvalī* Harṣa gives to the emperor the epithet of *Sārvabhauma* [Act IV].

as his satellites. These have also certain special titles, such as *Mahārāja*, *Mahāsāmanta*, *Mahāpratihāra*, *Mahādaṇḍanāyaka*, and *Mahākartākṛitika*, all of which we see applied to Dhruvasena I of Valabhī for instance (A. D. 535) [*IA*, iv. 105]. We have already seen how these *Sāmanta rājās* or subordinate kings were always in attendance upon Harṣa and their suzerain and even fought his battles. Of a higher status than these *Sāmantas* were the *Pratyanta Nṛipatis*, as they are called in the Allahabad Inscription of Samudragupta.

From the feudatory chiefs were sometimes recruited the highest officers of the empire. An inscription gives the gradation of officials as Sāmanta—Bhogika—Viṣayapati [Grant of Jayabhaṭa II, *IA*, v. 114]. The Banskhera Inscription of Harṣa mentions Mahāsāmanta Mahārāja Bhāna, and the Madhuban Inscription, Mahāsāmanta Skandagupta and Sāmanta Mahārāja Īśvaragupta as the emperor's officials.

The inscriptions present a hierarchy of officers, and of administrative divisions to which they are assigned.

The territory of the empire was called a *rājya* (No. 55 of Fleet), a *rāṣṭra*, *deśa*, or *maṇḍala* (see Fleet for the references). It was made up of a number of administrative divisions which are not always the same in the inscriptions. More usually they appear to be as follows in the descending order: Bhukti—Viṣaya—Grāma. In the Dāmodarpur plates the Gupta empire appears divided into a number of *Bhuktis* or provinces, one of which is named as

Puṇḍravardhana, which again was subdivided into a number of Viṣayas of which Koṭivarṣa (probably parts of Rajshahi, Dinajpur, Malda, and Bogra districts) is named as one. The Viṣaya had its administrative head-quarters called Adhiṣṭhāna or town. An inscription of A.D. 766 [No. 39 of Fleet] gives the series *grāma—paṭhaka—āhāra* [same as *Viṣaya* and first used in the Asokan edicts]. Other inscriptions consider the *grāma* as part of a *Santaka* or a *Peṭha* (see Fleet). The Madhuban Inscription of Harṣa mentions the *grāma* of Somakundakā belonging to the *Viṣaya* of Kuṇḍadhānī in the *Bhukti* of Śrāvastī, while the Banskhera Plate mentions the Ahichchhatra *Bhukti* in his empire.[1]

We shall now consider the officers assigned in the inscriptions to these administrative divisions. First comes the governor of the province designated as *Uparika-mahārāju* in the Damodarpur inscriptions. To this highest office was sometimes appointed even the king's son. The Emperor Bhānugupta, imitating the system of the Mauryan emperors, appointed his son named Devabhaṭṭāraka, and designated in the inscription [*Ep. Ind.* xv. 142] as *Uparika-mahārāja rājaputra*, to the headship of the province or the *bhukti* of Puṇḍravardhana. The governor is also called by other names such as *Goptā*[2] [No. 14 of

[1] Some of the names of the *Bhuktis* of the Gupta empire are given in the epigraphic records; e. g., Tīrabhukti, Puṇḍravardhana-bhukti, and Nagara Bhukti.

[2] '*Sarveṣu deśeṣu vidhāya Goptṛīn.*' Here the term *Deśa* stands for the province or *Bhukti*; other examples of this use are

Fleet], *Bhogika* (already referred to), *Bhogapati* [*Harṣa-charita* (237)], *Rājasthānīya* (literally, a Viceroy), and *Rāṣṭriya* [in Rudradāman's Junāgaḍh inscription] or *Rāṣṭrapati* [*IA*, vii. 63].

The provincial governor appointed his subordinate officials, described as being *tan-niyuktakas*. He appointed his *Viṣayapati* (or the divisional commissioner) to whom the Damodarpur inscriptions apply the titles of *Kumārāmātya*[1] [lit. the counsellor for a prince appointed as governor as distinguished from the *Rājāmātya* (No. 46 of Fleet)] and *Āyuktaka*, also used in *Harṣa-charita* (237). We have also the terms *Āyuktapuruṣa* [in the Allahabad Pillar Inscription of Samudragupta] and *Viniyuktaka* [No. 38 of Fleet, where it is mentioned after the *āyuktakas* to indicate its inferior status]. Probably these were general terms for all government servants [cf. the *Yuktas* of Asokan edict]. The Madhuban Plate of Harṣa gives the following series of higher officers: *Mahāsāmantas, Mahārājas, Daussādhasādhanikas, Pramātāras, Rājasthānīyas, Kumārāmātyas, Uparikas*, and *Viṣayapatis*.

As has been already stated, the *Viṣayapatis* had their head-quarters in the *adhiṣṭhānas* or 'civil stations' in which were located their own *adhi*-

Sukulideśa, Surāṣṭra-deśa, or Dabhālā-deśa of the Gupta Inscriptions. Similarly, the term *Pradeśa* is sometimes used for *Viṣaya*, e. g., Arikiṇa called a *Pradeśa* in the Eran Inscription of Samudragupta.

[1] In the inscription on the Basārh seal appears the full title of the office, viz. *Yuvarājapādīyakumārāmātyādhikaraṇa*.

karaṇas, their offices or courts. An inscription on one of the Basārh seals refers to the district office of Vaiśālī (*Vaiśālyādhiṣṭhānādhikaraṇa*). We read of the *Drāṅgikas* or the city magistrates (No. 38 of Fleet), and of a provincial governor appointing his son in charge of a city [No. 14]. The staff of the local government also included the following officers mentioned in different inscriptions: the *Mahattaras* (the village elders), the *Aṣṭa-Kulādhikaraṇas*[1] (probably officers in charge of groups of eight kulas or families in the village), and the *Grāmikas* (the village head-men) [Damodarpur plates]; the *Śaulkika* (in charge of tolls or customs), the *Gaulmika* (in charge of forests or perhaps forts; Manu uses the word *gulma* for a fort), and the *Agrahārika* (in charge of the *agrahāras* or villages dedicated to gods or Brahmins) [No. 12 of Fleet and also *Harṣa-charita* (237)]; the *Dhruvādhikaraṇas* (in charge of land-revenue) [No. 38 of Fleet]; the *Bhāṇḍāgārādhikṛita*, the treasurer [*Ep. Ind.* xii. 75]; the *Talavāṭaka*, probably the village accountant [No. 46 of Fleet]; the tax-collector, called *utkheṭa-yita* in an inscription of Bhāskaravarman [*Ep. Ind.* xii. 75], and, lastly, the notaries on whose keeping of records depended the stability of the administration, who are called *pustapālas* (in the Damodarpur inscriptions), *pustakakṛit* in *Harṣa-charita* (47), and *akṣapaṭalikas* attached to the Records office called *Akṣapaṭala*, under the departmental head called the *Mahākṣapaṭalika*

[1] Bāṇa refers to *Pañchakulaḥ adhyakṣaḥ* (p. 286, Bombay ed.).

[Nos. 39 and 60 of Fleet]. The Department of Records included the clerks who wrote down the records or documents. The writers are called the *Diviras* [No. 27], and *Lekhakas* [No. 80, *ibid.*], and the documents, the *Karaṇas* [No. 55, *ibid.*], kept in the custody of the registrar called *Karaṇika*. The *Harṣa-charita* calls a clerk *Karaṇi*, as we have already seen. The officer drafting the document is called the *Kartṛi* [No. 88 of Fleet] or *Śāsayitṛi* [Inscription of Bhāskaravarman, *Ep. Ind.* xii. 75]. The duties of these record-keepers were to know the titles and boundaries of lands, and report on them to government in the case of lands under proposal of transfer, that 'the lands may be given' (Damodarpur Inscriptions, 1 and 2) or that 'the application (for transfer of land) is a proper one' (*ibid.* 3). It was on their report that the government would sanction the sale of lands. The Damodarpur Inscriptions show that the government also consulted the other rural officers, the *Mahattaras*, the *Aṣṭakulādhikaraṇas*, and the *Grāmikas* in the inspection (*pratyavekṣya*) of the transactions relating to the transfer of land. Besides these officers with specified functions, there were also what are called 'general superintendents', *Sarvādhyakṣas* [No. 55 of Fleet], in whose offices were employed officers who were high-born, the kulaputras, evidently for the responsibility of their work. The *Harṣa-charita* also mentions *Adhyakṣas* (254).

Besides these officers, the machinery of Local Government provided a place also for the non-official element to help in the administration. The *Visaya-pati* administered with the assistance (*puroge saṃ-vyavaharati*) of an advisory council consisting of (1) the *Nagara-Śreṣṭhin*, perhaps as representing the city; (2) the *Sārthavāha* representing the trade guilds; (3) the *Prathama-kulika* representing the craft-guilds; and (4) the *Prathama-kāyastha*, the chief secretary, or the representative of the kāyasthas or scribes as a class, as the expert in respect of the documents to be referred to [Damodarpur Plate Inscriptions]. In the Madhuban Plate, Harṣa announces his grant of an agrahāra to two Sāmavedin and Rigvedin Brahmins in the presence of all his chief officers already mentioned and also of 'the regular and irregular troops', servants, and others, and 'the resident people' (*bhaṭachāṭusevakadīnprativāsija-napadāṁśchu*), who are called as witnesses to the transaction. This introduced a sort of democratic flavour to imperial administration.

When the king's orders were thus personally delivered, they were called *svamukhājñā*. Sometimes they were also signed by the king himself. The Banskhera Plate grant of Harṣa is signed by him and described as 'given under my own hand and seal'[1] (*svahasto mama mahārājādhirājaśrī Harṣasya*).

But more often the king's orders were delivered through the *Dūtakas*, *Dūtas*, or *Ājñādāpakas*, to the local officers, who would then draw up the necessary

1 Bāṇa calls a signet ring *Śāsana-valaya* (seal bracelet) [*HC*, p. 227 Bombay ed.].

charter and hand it over to the grantees or parties concerned [see Fleet for the references]. Thus the office of the *Dūta*, as the mouthpiece of the sovereign, was one of great trust and responsibility, and was, accordingly, given to the higher officers of the rank of a *Rājasthanīya* or an *Uparika* [*ibid.*]. The royal orders sanctioning grants of land were generally engraved on copper plates, the engraver being called the *Sekyakāra* [*Ep. Ind.* xii. 75].

Among other civil officers, we may note those attached to the royal household such as the *Pratīhāra*, the *Mahāpratīhāra* (the chief guard or usher of the palace), the *Vinayāsura*, whose function seems to have been to announce and conduct visitors to the king[1] [*Arch. Sur. Report*, 1903, p. 102], the *S'hapati-samrāṭ*, probably 'superintendent of the attendants of the women's departments' [No. 26 of Fleet; cf. *strī-adhyakṣa-mahāmātra* of the Asokan Edict], the *Pratinartaka* (No. 39 of Fleet), a bard or herald, and the like.

Law and order also claimed a variety of military and executive officers. The higher classes included *Mahāsenāpati* and *Senāpati*; *Mahābalādhikṛita* and *Balādhikṛita* also used in *Harṣa-charita* (228); *Mahābalādhyakṣa*, and *Balādhyakṣa*; *Bhaṭāśvapati*, commander of infantry and cavalry (mentioned in a Basārh Seal inscription); *Kaṭuka* [commander of elephants, mentioned in the *Harṣa-charita* (228)];

[1] Bāṇa calls the usher *Utsāraṇa*, and the chamberlain *Pratīhāra*, *Utsāraka*, and *Samutsāraka*.

and *Bṛihadaśvavāra*, 'head cavalry officer' (mentioned by Bāṇa); *Mahāsandhivigrahika* (officer to determine peace and war, and hence, Foreign Secretary) and *Sāndhivigrahika* [*Harṣa-charita* (217)]; *Mahāsarvadaṇḍanāyaka* and *Sarvadaṇḍanāyaka*; *Mahādaṇḍanāyaka*[1] (chief justice or chief executive officer to dispense punishments); *Daṇḍapāśika* (policeman), *Daṇḍika* and *Chauroddharaṇika* (officer apprehending thieves) [see Fleet for the references; specially No. 46]. One of the Basārh seals mentions a separate treasurer for the war office (*Raṇa-bhāṇḍāgārādhikaraṇa*), and an executive officer for enforcing discipline and morals called *Vinayasthitisthāpaka*. He was a provincial officer, mentioned in this epigraph as being appointed as censor for the whole province of Tirhut (*Tīrabhuktau*). The *Harṣa-charita* (228) speaks of 'superintendents of soldiers' barracks' called *Pāṭī-patis*, and also knows of 'women watchers of the night' called *Yāma-cheṭīs*.

Some of these high offices were combined in one and the same person. Hariṣeṇa, under Samudragupta, was at once his Sāndhivigrahika, Kumarāmātya, and Mahādaṇḍanāyaka. They were also held sometimes in heredity. The office of *Sachiva* (foreign

[1] The term *Mahādaṇḍanāyaka*, one of the commonest terms in the Gupta and later inscriptions, which has been in use for several centuries (from the fourth to the twelfth century as shown below), may be traced even to earlier times. It occurs, for instance, in a Mathurā Inscription of the Kushān Emperor Huviṣka [Inscription No. 3 in *JRAS*, 1924, p. 402, giving the latest reading of its text].

minister) under Chandragupta II was thus held as well as that of *Goptā* (governor) of Daśapura under Kumāragupta I [Nos. 6 and 18 of Fleet].

We may now consider the evidence regarding fiscal administration and specially the sources of revenue. These last may be gathered from the inscriptions recording the grants of land of the period. We may select for the purpose two typical grants for the years A.D. 571, and A.D. 766, between which lies the age of Harṣa [Nos. 38 and 39 of Fleet]. The former mentions as the sources of revenue (1) *udraṅga*, probably the land-tax; (2) *uparikara* ['a tax levied on cultivators who have no proprietary rights on soil' (Fleet)]; (3) *vāta* (unexplained); (4) *bhūta* (probably what is grown as distinguished from withered, *vāta*); (5) *dhānya*; (6) *hiraṇya* (gold); (7) *ādeya* (that to be surrendered); (8) *viṣṭika* (forced labour if necessary), to which the second inscription adds (9) *daśāparādhaḥ* [fines from ten offences, viz. (*a*) three offences of the *body*, theft, murder, and adultery; (*b*) four offences of *speech*, harsh words, untruthful words, libellous words, and pointless words; and (*c*) three offences of *mind*, coveting others' property, thinking of wrong, and devotion to what is not the true]; (10) *bhoga* (enjoyment); (11) *bhāga* (share). No. 55 of Fleet's *Gupta Inscriptions* indicates very well, though negatively, the obligations imposed by the state on a village rendered free by the king's grant: 'It is not to pay taxes (*akarādāyī*); it is not to be molested by the regular troops (*bhaṭa*) or police (*chhātra*); it is not to yield the increase in its cows and bulls; nor in its flowers or milk, pasturage, hide and charcoal, nor any taxes on salt or wet salt, on sale and purchase, or produce of mines; it is not to contribute forced labour or surrender its hidden treasures and deposits, the *klṛipta* and *upaklṛipta* (unexplained).' It would appear from this passage that even the best financial brain of modern times would be unable to improve upon the resources of taxation as explored and exploited in these olden times!

A sound system of local finance rested on a sound system of settlement'. An idea of the 'settlement' is given in No. 38 of Fleet of A.D. 571. Land was surveyed, measured, and divided into holdings called *pratyayas*[1] with their boundaries[2] defined. The measurement was by *pada* or pace, i.e., roughly two feet. The holdings were of different sizes, of 105, 100, and 90 *padāvartas*, and were served by common lands called *padraka* and had in certain cases the irrigation wells, *vāpi*, covering an area of 28 *padāvartas*. The names of all the individual proprietors of the holdings were entered in the village records together with the boundaries of the holdings which were fixed by a separate class of officers called *sīmākarmakara* [mentioned in No. 46 of Fleet], or *sīmāpradātā* [named in an inscription of Bhāskaravarman, *Ep. Ind.* xii. 75]. The officer surveying and

[1] Bāṇa calls small holdings *kedārikam*.

[2] Called *parihāra* and *maryādā* by Bāṇa.

measuring the land was called the *Pramātā*. There was also an officer called *Nyūya-karaṇika* [*ibid.*], 'the adjudicator who had to inspect and decide if the boundaries were properly marked out or not, and to settle all cases of dispute'.

As the village was the unit of administration, a census seems to have been taken of all the villages comprised in its territory. The Aihole Inscription of Pulakeśin II, Harṣa's great contemporary and rival, states that his empire of Mahārāṣṭra in its three divisions comprised as many as 99,000 villages.

The standard size of a village is also indicated in one inscription [No. 55 of Fleet], where it is stated that 'the village named Charmārika on the bank of the river Madhunadī in the Bhojakaṭa kingdom measured by 8,000 *bhūmis* according to the royal measure' was given to 1,000 Brahmins, so that an individual homestead would comprise 8 *bhūmis*.[1]

[1] If we look before and after (as we ought in history) a little further, we shall find that the names of most of these administrative officers had been in use from the time of the Guptas through that of Harṣa up to a still later period. For instance, an inscription assigned to the eleventh century A.D. [Belava Copper-plate Inscription of Bhojavarmadeva issued from the king's camp at Vikramapura in East Bengal (*Ep. Ind.* xii. 37)] mentions the following officers: Rājāmatya, Purohita, *Piṭhikāvitta* (unexplained), Mahādharmādhyakṣa (Chief Justice),[1] Mahāsandhivigrahika, Mahāsenāpati, *Mahāmudrādhikṛita* (Keeper of the Royal Seal), *Antaraṅgabṛhaduparika* [Chief Privy Councillor or Royal Physician—'Vidyākulasampanno hi viṣagantaraṅga ityuchyate' (Śivadāsa's commentary on Chakradatta)], Mahākṣapaṭalika, Mahāpratīhāra, Mahābhogika, *Mahāvyūhapati*, *Mahāpīlupati* (Chief Elephant Keeper), *Mahāgaṇastha* [Commander of a *gaṇa* squadron of 27 elephants, 27 chariots, 81 horses, and 135 foot soldiers; a *gulma* squadron compris-

Lastly, in connexion with his administration may be discussed the question of Harṣa's coins and the light they throw on his political status. Mr. R. Burn, C.S.I., I.C.S., has described [*JRAS.*, 1906,

ing 9 elephants, 9 chariots, 27 horses, and 45 foot-soldiers], Dauss-ādhika (Porter or Superintendent of villages), Chauroddharaṇika, Inspectors of the fleet, elephants, horses, cows, buffaloes, goats, sheep, &c., Gaulmikas, Daṇḍapāśikas, Daṇḍanāyakas, Viṣayapati, and other dependants of the king mentioned in the standard list of *Adhyakṣas.* The names of those officers are also repeated word for word in another slightly later inscription, the Naihati Grant of Vallāla Sena [*Ep. Ind.* xiv. 160]. Of these names, only the few in italics are new ones. It may be further noted that in these inscriptions, while the term for the province is still the old Gupta word *Bhukti*, there are new terms employed for the administrative divisions between the Bhukti and the Grāma, viz. the *Maṇḍala* (district or circle) and the *Khaṇḍala* (subdivision).

Again, it is clear from the above account of the Imperial Administrative System of this age, that we have left far behind the age of the Mauryan Imperial System as described in the Arthaśāstra of Kauṭilīya, or the Edicts of Asoka, or other documents, where the technical terms used for the various officers or departments of administration are mostly very different from, and more archaic than, those in use under the later administrations. As examples, we may recall Kauṭilīya's names for the eighteen *Tīrthas* or Chief Officers of the State such as the Mantrī, Purohita, Senāpati, Yuvarāja, Dauvārika, Antarvaśika, Praśāstṛi, Samāhartṛi, Sannidhātṛi, Pradeṣṭṛi, Nāyaka, Pauravyāvahāraka, Kārmāntika, Mantripariṣadadhyakṣa, Daṇḍapāla, Durgapāla, Antapāla, and Āṭavika; or the names of the local and rural officers like the *Gopa* and *Sthānika*; or the various classes of officers serving as secret agents (gūḍhapuruṣas) in the organization of espionage which was such a marked feature of the Mauryan government; or, lastly, such names of officers as Mahāmātra, Dharma-Mahāmātra, Strī-adhyakṣa-Mahāmātra, Anta-Mahāmātra, Rājūka, Prativedaka, Prādeśika, and the Yukta, which we find mentioned in the Asokan Edicts. No doubt the *functions* of administration remained nearly the same from age to age, but the functionaries differed as regards their names and spheres of work.

p. 843 f.] a find of silver coins out of which nine are of Śra Pratapaśala = Śrī Pratāpaśīla, 284 of Śrī-Śaladata, i.e., Śīlāditya, and one of Harśa (not spelt as Harṣa). The full legend of these Śīlāditya coins reads as follows: 'Vijitāvanir-avanipati Śrī Śīlāditya divam jayati', Śrī Śīlāditya, the conqueror, and master, of the world conquers Heaven. Thus these Pratāpaśīla and Śīlāditya coins[1] may be taken to be those issued by Pratāpaśīla, the name earned by King Prabhākaravardhana by his conquests, as Bāṇa informs us, and also the coins issued by his son Harṣa who was also known by his title of Śīlāditya, as Yuan Chwang informs us. This ascription of the coins is, however, doubted by Dr. Hoernle [*JRAS*, 1909, p. 446 f.] on the grounds (1) that the Kashmir Chronicle [ch. iii, v. 330] knows of a Pratāpaśīla, also called Śīlāditya, who was the son of Vikramāditya whom he identifies with Yaśodharman, the leader of the confederacy against the tyranny of Mihirakula, the Hūṇa (A.D. 528), and (2) that the *Harṣa-charita* does *not* know of the title Śīlāditya being assumed by Harṣa. Though there is some force in these objections, it does not render inadmissible Mr. Burn's conclusion, which is supported by several strong considerations: first, the identity of Pratāpaśīla with Prabhākaravardhana, as asserted by Bāṇa; second, the identity of Śīlāditya with Harṣa, as asserted by Yuan Chwang, a hardly less trust-

[1] On some of these coins Mr. Burn [*JRAS*, 1906, p. 850] reads the dates 31 and 33.

worthy chronicler than Bāṇa; third, the legends on the coins pointing to the status of kings like Prabhākara and Harṣa; fourth, the *provenance*[1] of the coins, all found within the limits of Harṣa's direct dominion and in association with the coins of the allied house of the Maukharis. To these may be added the further consideration that the type of these coins, showing a large head on one side and a peacock on the other (with long inscriptions), also agrees with that of the coins of Īśānavarman and other Maukhari kings and is modelled on the Gupta coin-types. Dr. Hoernle is, however, sure about one other coin being that of Harṣa [*JRAS*, 1903, p. 547]: it is the coin No. 21 given in Plate V of Cunningham's *Coins of Mediaeval India*, showing, on the obverse, the figure of a horseman, with the legend *Harṣa Deva*, and, on the reverse, that of a goddess seated on a throne with the cornucopiae in her left hand. Harṣa is called Harṣa Deva in the *Harṣa-charita* as well as in some inscriptions such as the Nausārī grant and the Aphsad Stone Inscription [*IA*, xiii. 73, 79]. The emblem of the 'Horseman with lance at rest' is taken by Hoernle to be 'the mark of the early Rājputs, i.e., the Hinduized Kushans, Hūṇas, and other invaders, and

[1] This is, however, as a rule the weakest argument for proving the point. Coins and copper-plates, being small and portable, are liable to be carried to places far from those of their origin, and are hence much inferior evidence in this regard as compared with stone-inscriptions. As an instance, we may point to the seal of the Maukhari king Śarvavarman found at Aśīrgaḍh, a village in the Nīmaḍ district of the Central Provinces, and hence hundreds of miles remote to the west from the place of its origin.

the chiefs of Thanesar were Rājputs' [*Ep. Ind.* i. 68]. The general type of the coin, which is a gold coin, with the enthroned goddess, corresponds to that in use among the Great and Little Kushans ruling from the third to the seventh century A.D. in Gandhara and the Panjab.

Besides coins, Harṣa also issued his seals, two of which were recently unearthed by excavations at Nālandā in fragments, and bearing inscriptions very much mutilated. The inscriptions on both mention '(para)ma Māheśvaraḥ Maheśvaraiva sārvva (bhaumaḥ) (paramabha) ṭṭāraka Mahārājādhirāja Śrī Harṣaḥ' and evidently recited the names of Harṣa's predecessors and ancestors whose names, except that of Rājyavardhana, are lost on the broken seals [Arch. Survey Report, Eastern Circle, 1917–18, p. 44]. The other seal known of Harṣa is, of course, the well-known Sonpat Copper Seal which, originally, was a part of a copper-plate, as shown by traces of soldering left on its back. The seal also shows at the top a bull recumbent to the proper right (the same symbol as is found on the Maukhari seals of Nālandā described above).

CHAPTER V

RELIGION AND LEARNING

FROM an account of the reign and administrative system of Harṣa, we now pass on to consider the state of the country during his time, for which, fortunately, ample evidence is available in the record of Yuan Chwang's travels. Yuan Chwang gives an admirable report on the Moral and Material Progress of India during that age, from which, voluminous as it is, we can but make only a few extracts for purposes of a general view.

The very visit of the Chinese pilgrim is a testimony to the moral progress and greatness achieved by India. It was not a mere pleasure trip upon which he came out to India. He came on a sacred and spiritual mission as a seeker after the saving knowledge of which India had then the monopoly in the whole of Asia. Thus no amount of dangers and difficulties presented by nature and man alike in the course of travelling by the land-route from China to India could damp the enthusiasm of Yuan Chwang and so many Chinese scholars before him for Indian learning and wisdom. Indeed from the time of Kaniṣka to that of Dharmapāla of Bengal, during the period of wellnigh ten centuries, there had been a steady stream of Chinese students towards India, towards her many seats of learning where they could drink at the very fountains of the wisdom they sought. The history of this cultural contact of China with India is only embodied in the three most conspicuous exponents and representatives of that movement, viz. Fa-hien, Yuan Chwang, and I-tsing, among numerous other students unknown to fame. Their pilgrimage to India is only a tribute paid by China to the sovereignty of Indian thought, whose influence extended beyond the geographical boundaries of India to many foreign countries and thus built up a Greater India beyond her northern mountains and southern seas.

Though Yuan Chwang was interested only in Buddhism, and that in one of its schools or sects, the Mahāyāna Buddhism, he has freely reported on the conditions as regards other Buddhist schools and sects as well as Brahminical systems of religion and culture then prevailing in the country. It would appear that Brahminism was then ascendant under the impetus given to it by the Gupta emperors. Yuan Chwang tells us that India was then known to foreigners as 'the country of the Brahmins', who were 'purest and in most esteem among the various castes and clans of the country' [Watters, i. 140]. The predominance of Brahminism was further demonstrated by the fact noticed by the Chinese pilgrim that Sanskrit was the language of the cultured classes in which wrote even the most famous Buddhist teachers. The best Sanskrit of the times, both spoken and written, was current in 'Mid-India' where the people were 'pre-eminently explicit and correct in speech, their expressions being harmonious and elegant, and their intonation clear and distinct, serving as rule and pattern for others'. Outside 'Mid-India' there were variations from the original source and standard. 'The people of neighbouring territories and foreign countries repeating errors until these became the norm, and emulous for vulgarities, have lost the pure style' [*ibid.* 153]. The vigour of Brahminism further expressed itself in the numerous ascetic sects of the times distinguishable from one another by external marks: 'Some wear peacocks' tails; some adorn themselves with a necklace of skulls; some are quite naked; some cover the body with grass or boards; some pull out their hair and clip their moustaches; some mat their side-hair and make a top-knot coil. Their cloth is not fixed and the colour varies' [*ibid.* 148]. There were also some who 'smeared themselves with ashes' [*ibid.* ii. 47], as well as those called Digambaras, Pāṁśupatas [*ibid.* i. 123]. The numerous Brahminical sects and schools of thought are also mentioned by Bāṇa as follows: viz., 'followers of Kṛiṣṇa, ascetics who pulled out their hair, followers of Kapila, Kanāda, the Nyāya and the Upaniṣads, the Lokāyatikas, and so forth.' In another passage Bāṇa mentions ascetic widows, Pārāśara mendicants, Jain monks, and Śaiva devotees as among his friends (48). Elsewhere he mentions such varieties of ascetics as the Karpaṭin (ragged ascetic), Kāṣṭha-muni (hermit on a pillar), Dagdhamuṇḍa, Pāṇḍurin and Piṇḍapātin. There were also the worshippers of Śiva and Śakti, the Kāpālika sect [*Life*, p. 159], and the devotees of Durgā [*ibid.*, p. 87]. The 'different heretical schools' are elsewhere thus described by Yuan Chwang [*ibid.*, p. 161]: 'The Bhūtas, Nirgranthas, the Kāpālikas and the Jutikas or Chudiṅkas (ascetics with matted hair) are all differently arrayed. The Śāṅkhyas and the Vaiśeṣikas are mutually opposed. The Bhūtas cover themselves with cinders . . . the Nirgranthas go without clothing . . . the sect of the Kāpālikas with their chaplets of bones round their heads and necks, inhabiting holes and crevices of the rocks. . . . As for the Chingkias (*Chudiṅkas*), they wear garments soiled with filth, and eat putrid food.'

But the external marks of these various classes of ascetics were certainly less characteristic than their inner marks. The Chinese pilgrim is quite eloquent about these:

'There are men who, far seen in antique lore and fond of the refinements of learning, are content in seclusion, leading lives of continence. These come and go outside of the world and promenade through life away from human affairs. Though they are not moved by honour or reproach, their fame is far spread.

'Though their family be in affluent circumstances, such men make up their minds to be like vagrants and get their food by begging as they go about. With them there is honour in knowing truth and there is no disgrace in being destitute.

'The rulers treating them with ceremony and respect cannot make them come to court. Now as the state holds men of learning and genius in esteem, and the people respect those who have high intelligence, the honours and praises of such men are conspicuously abundant, and the attentions, private and official, paid to them are very considerable. Hence men can force themselves to a thorough acquisition of knowledge.'

One of the best proofs of the moral progress of India was this growth of asceticism and the way in which it was esteemed and encouraged both by the rulers and the people at large. India could show in abundance men who renounced riches, the comforts of home, the many pleasures of social life and even the love of fame ('that last infirmity of noble minds'), as so many impediments to the quest of Truth. And the moral sense of a society was strong and sound that showed all honour to those who thus beggared themselves for the uplift of society. For the ascetics were not against social service: they left the world to give the law unto the world. Attaining Truth, they were anxious to impart it to their fellows. This fact did not escape the observation of Yuan Chwang who remarks:

'Forgetting fatigue, they "expatiate in the arts and sciences"; seeking for wisdom while "relying on perfect virtue" they count not 1,000 *li* a long journey' (1 *li* = about 4 miles) [Watters, i. 161].

Thus in these travelling bands of ascetic teachers, ancient India found one of the best agencies of public instruction without any expense to the state which could not have tackled the problem in such an efficient manner departmentally.

Side by side with the various sects and schools of Brahminism flourished those of Buddhism and especially of Mahāyāna Buddhism, which in Yuan Chwang's time had proportionately extended more than Hīnayāna. Thus, at every centre of Buddhism he visited, he noticed both Mahāyāna and Hīnayāna monks living sometimes even in the same and sometimes in different monasteries, together with numerous 'Deva-temples' and Brahminical sects and devotees 'living pell-mell'.

Buddhism at the time of Harṣa and Yuan Chwang, though on the wane, was still represented by as many as eighteen different sects, besides its main division into Mahāyāna and Hīnayāna. 'The tenets of the schools keep these isolated, and controversy runs high; heresies on special doctrines lead many ways to the same end. Each of the eighteen schools claims to have intellectual superiority' [Watters, i. 162]. Some of these schools developed special literature of their own bearing upon their particular tenets and practices and also owned monasteries where it was specially cultivated. Between the various schools there were about 5,000 monasteries seen by the Chinese pilgrim in India in working order as so many Buddhist colleges where Buddhist monks were in actual residence, of whom the total number all over India, including Ceylon, works out to be something like 212,130 on the basis of Yuan Chwang's totals for different sects and monasteries in different centres.

The following table has been prepared from the statements of Yuan Chwang to show the distribution of monks among the different schools and centres of Buddhism in India in the age of Harṣa:

1. *Sthavira:*

In Gayā (in the Vihāra of the Ceylonese king)	1,000
,, Samataṭa	2,000
,, Kaliṅga	500
,, Dravida	10,000
,, Ceylon	20,000
,, Bharoach	300
,, Surat	3,000
Total	36,800

2. *Sammatīya:*

In Ahichchhatra	1,000
,, Saṅkāśya	1,000
,, Hayamukha	1,000
,, Viśoka	3,000
,, Kapilavastu	30
,, Benares	3 000
,, Sārnāth	1,500
,, Monghyr	4,000
,, Karṇasuvarṇa	2,000
,, Mālava	20,000
,, Valabhī	6,000
,, N. Sindh	10,000
,, Karachi	5,000
,, Pitāśilā	3,000
,, Avanda (?)	2,000
,, Ānandapura	1,000
Total	63,530

3. *Sarvāstivādin* :

In Gaz	2,000
,, Tamasāvana Vihāra	300
,, Matipur	800
,, Pigeon Vihāra	200
,, Navadevakula	500
,, Gurjara	100
,, Monghyr	2,000
Total	4,100

4. *Lokottaravādin* :

In Bamian	(several thousands)

5. *Hīnayāna* (without mention of any sects) :

In Śākala	100
,, Gandhāra	50
,, Sthāneśvara	700
,, Śrughna	1,000
,, Goviśāna	100
,, Kosambi	300
,, Ghazipur	1,000
,, Magadha	50
,, Champā	200
Total	3,500

6. *Mahāyāna* :

In Kapis	6,000
,, Udyāna	18,000
,, Takṣaśilā	300
,, Ku-lu-to (on the Upper Beas)	1,000
,, Pi-lo-shan-na	300
,, Magadha	10,000
,, Puṇyavardhana	700
,, Orissa	'Myriads'
,, S. Kośala	10,000
,, Ti-lo-shi-ka Vihāra	1,000
,, Dhanakaṭaka	1,000
,, Fa-la-na (Gomal valley)	300
Total	48,600

7. Bhikṣus who studied both Hīnayāna and Mahāyāna:

In Mathurā	2,000
,, Jālandhara	2,000
,, Kanyākubja	10,000
,, Ayodhyā	3,000
,, Vṛiji	1,000
,, Puṇyavardhana	3,000
,, Kaṅkana	10,000
,, Mahārāṣṭra	5,000
,, Cutch	1,000
,, Ujjeni	300
,, Parvata	1,000
,, Mókran	6,000
Total	46,300

8. Bhikṣus whose sects are not specified:

In Kashmir	5,000
,, Rajmahal	300
,, Tāmralipti	1,000
,, Andhra	3,000
Total	9,300

Totals of above:

Hīnayāna:		
Sthavira	36,800	
Sammatīya	63,530	
Sarvāstivādin	4,100	
Unnamed	3,500	
		107,930
Mahāyāna		48,600
Both Hīnayāna and Mahāyāna		46,300
Monks whose sects are not specified		9,300
Grand Total		212,130[1]

[1] The above computation is based on that of Rhys Davids [*JRAS*, 1891, pp. 418–20], from which, however, it differs as regards several figures taken from Watters.

It may be noted that there were, besides, many other monks and monasteries not counted by Yuan Chwang but only vaguely estimated by the words 'few', 'some tens', 'several thousands', or 'myriads'. Thus, granting that Yuan Chwang's census of Buddhist monks cannot be expected to be absolutely accurate, it cannot be denied that India supported quite a considerable number, several lacs, of ascetics of both Buddhist and non-Buddhist orders, which cannot but be taken as a convincing proof of her moral and spiritual progress in a particular direction.

It may be useful to note the most important of the Buddhist colleges as observed by Yuan Chwang. Kashmir could boast of being a great centre of Buddhism where the king appointed Bhadanta Ch'êng with his disciples to look after the needs of the pilgrim and twenty clerks to copy out the manuscripts he wanted from the Palace Library. He thus spent two years there, studying certain sūtras and śāstras. In the Nagaradhana Vihāra of Jālandhara country he spent four months in study under a learned scholar, Chandravarmā. In a monastery in the Śrughna country he spent a whole winter and half of the spring in receiving instruction under the learned scholar Jayagupta. The monasteries in the Śrughna country were so famous for the erudition of their monks that distinguished monks from other lands came to them to have their doubts solved. In a monastery in Matipur he saw a learned scholar, Mitrasena by name, ninety years old, and a disciple of Guṇaprabha, one of whose works he studied there for several months. The Bhadravihāra was a noted college in Kanyākubja where Yuan Chwang stayed for three months, studying under the teacher Vīryasena. In the Śvetapura monastery in the Vaiśāli country the pilgrim obtained a copy of the Mahāyāna treatise. The Ti-lo-shi-ka monastery near Nālandā was then 'the rendezvous of eminent scholars who flocked to it from all regions'. The Mahābodhi monastery at Gayā was distinguished for the perfection in the Vinaya observances on the part of all its 1,000 ecclesiastics. One of the monasteries of Puṇyavardhana attracted by its reputation many distinguished students from 'East India'. In Monghyr the pilgrim stayed for a year receiving instruction from the teachers, Tathāgatagupta and Kṣāntisiṁha. The Raktāmṛita monastery in Karṇasuvarṇa was the resort of illustrious brethren. Thus all these monasteries were then enjoying almost an all-Indian reputation as seats of Buddhist learning and culture.

But of course the most distinguished centre of learning in that age was the far-famed university of Nālandā, which then counted 10,000 students on its rolls. Even 'foreign students came there to put an end to their doubts and then become celebrated' [Watters, ii. 165]. Some of these came even from Mongolia [I-tsing, ed. Takakusu, p. 26]. The history of this university needs special treatment, but here it is relevant only to notice such facts and conditions as are connected with the time of Harṣa. Residence for 10,000 alumni was provided in six-storied monasteries, the gift of six kings, namely, Śakrāditya, Buddhagupta, Tathāgatagupta, Bālāditya, Vajra, and a king of Mid-India. Harṣa's gift to the university was a Vihāra or temple of brass or bronze about a hundred feet in height [*Life*, p. 159; Watters, ii. 171]. The university provided for its alumni not only free education but also free board, lodging, clothes, bedding, and medicines. Its expenses came out of its estates. 'The king of the country', says Yuan Chwang, 'remitted the revenues of 100 villages for the endowment of the convent', but he does not mention the name of this generous king. The university, comprising only 'Schools of Discussion', was meant not for elementary instruction but for advanced studies and students. The method of learning there was mainly by discussion for which but few were fit. Yuan Chwang says that only two or three out of ten could succeed in gaining admission to the university and its 'Schools of Discussion'; 'the majority beaten by the difficulties of the problems (they had to answer before admission) withdrew'. And yet such advanced scholars who got admitted he counts as 10,000! [*ibid.* 165]. Of these, 1,510 were teachers who between them delivered 100 different discourses on different subjects every day.

The teachers and students at Nālandā were exponents and followers of different sects or schools of thought, and were always meeting in animated debates and discussions which so largely made up the intellectual life of the university. Yuan Chwang records a few actual cases of such discussions. Once, while he was deputed by Śīlabhadra to expound some aspects of Yoga-śāstra, another learned man named Siṁharaśmi was discoursing on quite contrary doctrines when he silenced him by his questions and drove him in shame to leave the convent and repair to the Bodhi monastery at Gaya, thence to bring his fellow-student, Chandrasiṁha of Eastern India, to Nālandā for discussion with Yuan Chwang, but Yuan Chwang prevailed over him at once. We are also told of a Lokāyata philosopher who came to challenge the Nālandā monks, 'wrote out forty theses and hung them up at the gate of the Vihāra with the notice: "If any one within can refute these principles, I will then give my head as a proof of his victory." Yuan Chwang accepted the challenge, got the poster removed, and, in the presence of the Chancellor, and all students, overcame by a learned discussion his opponent who, spared his head, became his disciple' [*Life*, pp. 157–64].

The most distinguished scholars and teachers of the times were 'Dharmapāla (the predecessor of Śīlabhadra in the headship of the establishment), Chandrapāla who gave a fragrance to Buddha's teachings, Guṇamati and Sthiramati of excellent reputation among contemporaries, Prabhāmitra of clear argument, and Jinamitra of elevated conversation, Jñānachandra of model character and perspicacious intellect, and Śīlabhadra', by far the most learned man of his time. Besides these specially mentioned, there 'were some thousands of Brethren, all men of great ability and learning, several hundreds being highly esteemed and famous'. Life at Nālandā was lived at high pressure: 'Learning and discussing they found the day too short; day and night they admonished each other, juniors and seniors mutually helping to perfection.'

The subjects of study at Nālandā were not confined to Buddhism alone. Though the university specialized in the study of Mahāyāna, it did not exclude the study of the works belonging to the eighteen other sects of Buddhism, nor of such Brahminical sacred and secular subjects as the Vedas, the Atharva Veda, Hetuvidyā (logic), Śabdavidyā (grammar and philology) Chikitsāvidyā (medicine), Sāṅkhya, Nyāya, Yoga-śāstra and the like. Yuan Chwang himself studied Yoga-śāstra under Chancellor Śīlabhadra, 'the highest living authority on the subject', as well as Nyāya, Hetuvidyā, and Śabdavidyā, including philological, legal, philosophical, and astronomical subjects together with the grammar of Pāṇini. He remained as a student at Nālandā for five years, during which he completed a study of 'all the collections of Buddhist books as well as the sacred book of the Brahmins' [*Life*, pp. 112, 121, 125]. Thus Nālandā stood for the ideal of freedom in learning, and welcomed knowledge from all quarters, from all sects and creeds. It was a genuine university in the *universal* range of its studies and not a mere sectarian, denominational school.

Comparable to Nālandā in the freedom of its academic life and the variety and catholicity of its studies, as described by Yuan Chwang, there was another seat of learning, the hermitage of the sage Divākaramitra, described by Bāṇa (*265, 266*). To that solitary and sylvan retreat in the depths of the Vindhyan forests was attracted all the varied learning and culture of the age. Students differing widely and radically in doctrines and practices, followers of all possible sects and schools of thought, gathered together in a common fellowship in the quest of Truth, the supreme object of a university. They were all busy 'pondering, urging objections, raising doubts, resolving them, giving etymologies, disputing, studying, and explaining'. Truth was, indeed, sought to be seen here from every conceivable view-point! There were the different sects of Jains, the Ārhatas (Digambara) and Śvetapaṭas (Śvetāmbaras); different classes of Brahminical ascetics such as Pāṭūrabhikṣus (naked ascetics), the Maskarins (parivrājaka), the Varṇins (brahmachārins), the Bhāgavatas and Pāñcharātrikas (Vaiṣṇava ascetics), the Śaivas and Keśaluñchakas; atheists like the Lokāyatikas (Chārvākas), philosophers like the Kāpilas, Kāṇādas, Aupaniṣadas (Vedāntins), and Aiśvarakāraṇikas (Naiyāyikas); experts in law (Dharmaśāstra), linguistics (Śābdika), and the Purāṇas; experts in rituals (Sāptatantavas); and even experts in the material sciences, the metallurgists (Kārandhamins). Nor were Buddhist learning and culture less in evidence there: the followers of the Three Refuges (Triśaraṇa) were busy performing the ritual of the chaitya (*chaitya-karma*); there were students well versed in the *Śākya-śāsanas* (Buddhist law): discourses were also forthcoming on Vasubandhu's Koṣa or Bauddhasiddhānta; while there were others who specialized in the study of the 'Bodhisattva-Jātakas' which they were always muttering.

We have in these accounts of educational institutions an indication of the literature and circle of knowledge available in that age. 'The Brahmans learnt the Veda treatises', including the Āyur Veda, Yajur Veda, Sāma Veda, and Atharva Veda, as stated by Yuan Chwang (Watters, i. 159). According to I-tsing, who travelled in India a little later than Yuan Chwang (A.D. 672–688), 'the Four Vedas containing about 100,000 verses have been handed down from mouth to mouth, not transcribed on paper or leaves. In every generation there exist some intelligent Brahmans who can recite the 100,000 verses' [Takakusu's tr., p. 182]. As noticed by I-tsing, the first book of reading was called *Siddhirastu*, giving the 49 letters of the alphabet and 10,000 syllables arranged in 300 slokas. After this the student was introduced to elementary grammar, comprising (*a*) the Sūtra of Pāṇini in 1,000 slokas, (*b*) *Dhātu* and the three *Khilas*, (*c*) the commentary on Pāṇini, called the *Kāśikāvṛitti*, in 18,000 slokas, of which the author Jayāditya, 'of great ability and striking literary power', flourished in the time of

Harṣa; (*d*) composition in prose and verse. After this preliminary grounding in grammar and composition, students could proceed to a study of *subjects* or Vidyās, which, according to both Yuan Chwang and I-tsing, were five in number, viz. (1) Śabdavidyā (grammar and lexicography), (2) Śilpasthānavidyā (the science of the arts and crafts), (3) Chikitsāvidyā (medicine), (4) Hetuvidyā (logic), and (5) Adhyātmavidyā (metaphysics). I-tsing mentions some of the text-books prescribed under these subjects. Under *Hetuvidyā*, for instance, the text-book used was the Nyāya-dvāra-tāraka-śāstra written by Nāgārjuna. As models of composition and standard literature are mentioned the Jātakamālā, the *Suhṛillekha* of Nāgārjuna, an epistle in verse addressed to his patron, King Jetaka Śātavāhana [Takakusu, p. 159], which was translated by I-tsing, and also the *Buddha-stotra* in 150 verses, which was also translated by I-tsing while he was studying at Nālandā. The study of these five subjects was followed by specialization. According to Yuan Chwang, the Buddhist student would specialize in the study of some branch of the religious literature connected with the sect to which he belonged. We are told of the famous Buddhist scholar Guṇabhadra who, in addition to these five subjects, knew astronomy, arithmetic, medicine, and exorcism [Watters, i. 158]. One of the subjects of specialization was *Vyākaraṇa*, under which the following text-books were then in use, as stated by I-tsing, viz. (1) *Chūrṇi* or Patañjali's Mahābhāṣya in 24,000 slokas which 'advanced students take three years to learn'; (2) *Bhartṛihari-śāstra*, a commentary on the above work in 25,000 slokas, written by Bhartṛihari, 'famous throughout the five parts of India', who died in A.D. 651 [Takakusu, p. 180]; (3) *Vākyapadīya*, also by Bhartṛihari, 'a treatise on the Inference supported by the authority of the sacred teaching and on Inductive Arguments' (*ibid.*); and (4) *Pei-na* (probably Sanskrit Beḍa or Veḍa), a grammatical work of 3,000 slokas composed by Bhartṛihari, with a commentary portion in 14,000 slokas attributed to his contemporary, Dharmapāla. Among the sacred works of Buddhist literature in which the monks specialized at the monasteries, I-tsing mentions the *Tripiṭaka* [*ibid.*, p. 120], the Vinaya, the sūtras and śāstras (*ibid.*, p. 181), the two hymns of 150 and 400 verses attributed to Mātṛicheta, taught to monks throughout India (p. 157), and the *Buddha-charita-kāvya* of Aśvaghoṣa, 'which is widely read or sung throughout the five divisions of India, and the countries of the Southern Sea' (p. 166). Under *Yoga* were studied the *Yogāchārya-śāstra* and the eight śāstras of Asaṅga: under *Logic* are mentioned Jina's eight śāstras; while, under *Abhidharma*, I-tsing refers to six Pādas or treatises, and, under the *Āgamas*, four Nikāyas.

This is what the Chinese travellers report on the Indian literature of the times. We notice several names as specifically belonging to the history of Sanskrit literature in the time of Harṣa, viz. the names of Bhartṛihari, of the joint authors of the *Kāśikā*, viz. Jayāditya and Vāmana, and of Dharmapāla, who wrote the sloka portion of the *Beḍā-vṛitti* and was the predecessor of Śīlabhadra in the headship of the Nālandā college; Dharmakīrti, the logician [referred to in the *Vāsavadattā* (p. 235) and the Sarva-Darśana-Saṁgraha of Cowell (p. 24)]; Rāhūlamitra, chief monk of Eastern India at Tāmralipti, author of the Ratnakūṭa Sūtra; Chandra, author of a drama on Vessantara; Jinaprabha, Jñānachandra, Ratnasiṁha, teachers at Nālandā in I-tsing's time, together with such other Buddhist teachers and scholars, both at Nālandā and elsewhere, as have been mentioned by Yuan Chwang and referred to above. A leading man of letters of the age was, of course, Bāṇabhaṭṭa, the court poet of Harṣa himself, while Bāṇa himself mentions the vernacular poet (bhāṣākavi) Īśāna, the descriptive poet, Veṇībhārata, and the Prākṛita poet, Vāyuvikāra, as among the literary celebrities of the times. The great poet Bhāravi, author of *Kirātārjunīya*, also belonged to this age, since he already appears as famous in the Aihole Inscription of A. D. 634, while the absence of any reference to him by Bāṇa should not make him precede Bāṇa by a long interval [Keith's *Classical Sanskrit Literature*, p. 51]. To the same age are also assigned the poet Kumāradāsa who wrote the *Jānakīharaṇa* epic, for he seems to know the Kāśikāvṛitti of about A.D. 650; and also the famous poet Māgha, author of the *Śiśupālabadha* [*ibid.*, p. 54]. The romancist, Subandhu, was a little earlier than Bāṇa, who refers to his *Vāsavadattā* in the preface to the *Harṣa-charita*. The *Kādambarī* of Bāṇa, left unfinished by him, was finished by his worthy son Bhūṣaṇa Bhaṭṭa. We may further note another royal poet, 'almost a contemporary to a day of Harṣa himself', named *Mahendravikrama*, the Pallava king of Kāñchī, who wrote the play called the *Mattavīlāsa*, and ruled in the first quarter of the seventh century A.D.; also the court-poet of Harṣa's great southern contemporary and rival Pulakeśin II, Ravikīrti by name, who celebrates his patron's exploits in the Aihole Inscription of A.D. 634 in the form of a poem which compares Ravikīrti to Kālidāsa and Bhāravi, and shows him to be well up in the rules of the Alaṁkāra Śāstra, familiar with the *Raghuvaṁśa* of Kālidāsa, and almost unsurpassed in some of his *Utprekṣās*. Lastly, we may also mention among the men of letters of this age the poet Mayūra, father-in-law of Bāṇa, and author of a Sūryaśataka, a work of great merit, and Mātaṅga Divākara, of whom some poems are preserved [Keith's *Classical Sanskrit Literature*, p. 120].

Side by side with religion and learning as centred in these monasteries and hermitages noted for their strenuous discipline and intellectual life, we must consider the religion of the masses which, whether Brahminical or Buddhist, was given to the worship of idols enshrined in temples. The most popular deities of Brahminical religion at that time were Viṣṇu, Śiva, and the Sun. Yuan Chwang noticed temples of all the three gods at Kanyākubja, which was then a centre of both Brahmanism and Buddhism. Benares was then, as now, the most important place of Śaiva worship. Yuan Chwang noticed there more than 100 temples of Hindu gods at which the majority of the worshippers were Śivites, 'some cutting off their hair, some going about naked, or smeared with ashes'. In one temple he saw an image of the *deva* (probably the Śivaliṅgam) 'nearly 100 ft. high' [Watters, ii. 47]. Some of these temples existed even at prominent Buddhist centres. Yuan Chwang speaks of an Īśvara temple at Kapilavastu, the Bethlehem of Buddhism. Worship of Durgā, the consort of Śiva, was also popular. Yuan Chwang saw a Bhīmā Devī temple near Śālātura in the Panjab near the Śiva temple, attended by 'ash-smearing Tīrthikas' [i. 221]. There were temples also of Earth-god even at Bodh Gayā [ii. 124]. The most famous Sun temple was that at Multan, where 'the image was of gold ornamented with precious substances', and the daily worshippers counted 'constantly 1,000 pilgrims from various lands', with 'a constant succession of females performing music, with lights kept burning all night, incense and flowers continually offered', while 'the kings and grandees of all India gave precious substances as religious offerings, and erected free rest-houses, with food, drink, and medicine for the sick and needy' [ii. 254].

Buddhism also was equally marked by the worship of images liberally introduced into it by the Mahāyāna school. There were topes in all places, associated with incidents in the life, or enshrining the relics, of the Buddha, and even sometimes of his disciples. At Mathurā, for instance, Yuan Chwang noticed worship of images of Sāriputra, Maudgalaputra, Upāli, Ānanda, and Rāhūla [i. 302]. Fa-hien, in the fifth century, saw in the same locality topes erected even to the Buddhist Scriptures, to the Sūtras, the Vinaya, and the Abhidharma. A typical Mahāyāna monastery in Magadha is thus described by Yuan Chwang [ii. 105]: 'The middle temple had a stone image of the Buddha, 30 feet high; the left-hand one had an image of Tārā Bodhisattva; and the right-hand one had an image of Avalokiteśvara Bodhisattva.'

India was thus pre-eminently a land of temples and worship of images on which all her different religions appear to agree, however much they may differ as regards their doctrines and deities. In all the chief cities of India, as we shall see, Yuan Chwang noticed abundance of what he calls 'Deva-temples', along with the Buddhist structures, whether temples, topes, vihāras, or other monuments.

Much of the moral and religious progress of the country was of course bound up to some extent with the character and example shown by the reigning sovereign. Harṣa was an example to his people in his pursuit and patronage of religion and learning. But it must be noted that he did not begin as a Buddhist, nor did he, as a Buddhist, only patronize Buddhism to the exclusion of all other religions in a narrow spirit of sectarianism that would ill become an emperor having to deal with different creeds and communities. According to Bāṇa, his ancestral religion was connected with Śaivaism and Tāntrika worship. The citizens of the capital included worshippers of Chaṇḍī and Mahākāla. In the palace in his father's time were found people 'worshipping the family gods, performing the Six Oblation sacrifices, chanting the Mahā-Māyūrī hymn (i.e., Bauddhavidyā according to the commentator), completing the rites for keeping out the spirits by offerings, earnest Brahmins occupied in muttering Vedic texts, Śaivas bathing Virūpākṣa's image with thousands of vessels of milk', while 'Siva's temple resounded with the murmur of the Hendecad to Rudra' (170-1). Similarly, the announcement of the birth of Harṣa himself was followed by 'Vaitāna fires blazing up with flames in the courts of sacrificers, and white-clad Brahmins approaching with Veda on their lips[1] together with the family priest' (143). We are also told that Harṣa, before setting out on his conquests, 'with deep devotion offered worship to the adorable Nīlalohita' (i.e., Rudra-Śiva) (226). Thus the atmosphere of

[1] An idea of the religion as practised by the Brahmins of those days may be had from Bāṇa's own account of it. The day he started on his visit to Harṣa, he rose early, bathed, wore a piece of fresh and pure cotton cloth, with a rosary recited many times suitable Vedic mantras; worshipped the idol of Śiva by bathing it in milk and offering it flowers and incense; then sacrificed to Agni by oblations of ghee, made gifts to Brahmins and went round the cow before commencing the journey.

Brahminical religion and culture pervaded the palace. In the dramas *Ratnāvalī* and *Priyadarśikā*, attributed to Harṣa, the benedictory verses mention the chief deities of Brahmanism, viz. Śiva (also called Śambhu and Hara) with his attendants, the Gaṇas, Gaurī (or Girijā), Gaṅgā, Brahmā, Kṛiṣṇa and Lakṣmī, Sarasvatī, together with the minor figures like Kumāra, or Daśamukha, or Dakṣa. Even in his frankly Buddhist drama of *Nāgānanda*, which begins with an invocation to Buddha Jina, the Brahmanical deities, Gaurī and Garuḍa, are given an important place. And there are, besides, passages in these dramas (see note to Chap. V) exhibiting the king's interest in the performance of sacrifices by Brahmins as the sign of the people's progress and efficiency of administration. The Sonpat Copper Seal and Madhuban Plate inscriptions of Harṣa even describe his father as a devout worshipper of Āditya or Sun, and the upholder of Varṇāśrama-dharma. According to Bāṇa, the conversion to Buddhism of Harṣa and his sister took place only after the completion of his conquests, and this may be true, because a programme of wars and bloodshed would not be strictly consistent with a religion like Buddhism with its gospel of non-violence and peace. The conversion is attributed by Bāṇa to the influence of the Buddhist ascetic Divākaramitra, who lived in his hermitage in the Vindhyan forests, as we have already seen. The Inscriptions, however, regard his elder brother as the first convert in his family to Buddhism and frankly describe him as a *parama-Saugata*, i.e., a prime devotee of the Buddha and promoting public good like the Sugata. It was, however, Yuan Chwang who definitely gave both Harṣa and his sister their faith in Mahāyāna Buddhism by his discourse on its doctrines, and exposure of the deficiency of Hīnayāna, at the very first meeting between the emperor and the pilgrim. His enthusiasm for his new faith led him at once to organize the grand assembly at Kanauj to give publicity to the masterly treatise of Yuan Chwang on Mahāyāna and establish its supremacy over all other creeds of the times.

It was also on that occasion that Harṣa unfortunately exhibited some amount of bigotry and intolerance not in keeping with the general tenor of his policy and administration, or the wide-hearted charity that distinguished him as a man. At that assembly, as we have already seen, the emperor cast a slur on Brahminical religion in many ways: he and his vassal, Kumāra Rājā of Assam, personating Indra and Brahmā, the chief Brahminical gods, were in attendance upon the image of Buddha to exhibit the subserviency of the gods to the Buddha! Even within the fold of Buddhism he showed a bias against Hīnayāna by interdicting freedom of speech in opposition to the discourse on Mahāyāna by Yuan Chwang in the assembly, by an angry proclamation that 'whoever speaks against him, his tongue shall be cut out', though the royal wrath was provoked by a plot engineered by the followers of Hīnayāna. This proclamation had the effect of reducing what began as a parliament of Indian religions into a mere sectarian assembly, for 'the followers of error withdrew and disappeared, so that there had been no one to enter on the discussion' [*Life*, p. 180]. According to another account [Beal, i. 219], the king's intolerant attitude at the assembly was answered by a plot on his own life designed by Brahmins who were in revolt because, while the king 'exhausted his treasury in offerings to the Śramaṇas, they coming from a distance had scarcely been spoken to'.

But this exclusive patronage of Buddhism seems to have been only occasional and exceptional, and was not a part of his general policy. In the assembly at Prayāga which immediately followed that of Kanauj and was not, like the latter, a special assembly summoned in the interests of a particular religion, but a regular institution holding its sessions every five years, the king's open-handed liberality was shared by all classes, castes, creeds, and communities in the country. The royal invitation was extended equally to 'all the Śramaṇas and Brahmins of the five Indies, besides the poor, the orphans, and the destitute' [*Life*, p. 184], to partake of the king's phenomenal charities, though precedence in the order of their distribution was given to the Buddhists. On this occasion Harṣa gave a further proof of his freedom from any sectarian spirit by officially recognizing and honouring the images of the Brahminical deities of the Sun and Śiva along with that of the Buddha in deference to the then three most popular faiths of the times connected with them. The inscriptions of Harṣa record also his grants of villages to orthodox Rigvedin and Sāmavedin Brahmins who, according to Bāṇa (84), looked up to him as their 'ready servant'.[1]

Harṣa's special patronage of Buddhism is associated with several other institutions. He forcibly secured from Kashmir the tooth-relic of the Buddha which he enshrined in a monastery built by him to the west of Kanauj [*Life*, p. 181]. We have already referred also to his gift of a temple of bronze, a hundred feet high, to the Nālandā convent. While touring through Orissa, he noticed the prevalence of Hīnayāna, to overthrow which he sent for four good preachers of Mahāyāna from distant Nālandā. The four preachers who were selected for this deputation to Orissa were Sāgaramati, Prajñāraśmi, Siṁharaśmi, and Yuan Chwang [*Life*, p. 160].

Some of his other measures for the promotion of Buddhism are also indicated by the Chinese pilgrim. Once a year he summoned all the Buddhist monks together and for twenty-one days provided them with all their requisites according to the rules. He was also fond of bringing together the Buddhist monks for discussion and examination followed by gifts to the meritorious: the best he would advance to the Lion's Throne (i.e., the highest place) and honour as

[1] Harṣa seems to have had some touch with Christianity too. Dr. Edkins makes the statement that his court was visited by the Syrian Christians, Alopen, and his companions, in A.D. 639 [*Athenaeum*, July 3, 1880, p. 8].

his own teachers, from whom he would take his spiritual instructions. Others, if they were perfect in the observance of the ceremonial code, he would formally honour. But those who showed lapses in morality or monkish discipline he would banish from his presence and from the country too [Watters, i. 344].

The Chinese pilgrim further tells us that he erected thousands of topes, 'each about 100 feet high', on the banks of the Ganges, and monasteries at the sacred places of Buddhism. 'He also furnished the chapels and liberally adorned the common halls of the monasteries' [*ibid.*]. But very few of these monuments of Harṣa have been unearthed by archaeological exploration.

Lastly, we may say that his legislation forbidding the use of animal food throughout the Five Indies and the destruction of life under severe penalties was due to his interest in Buddhism.[1]

[1] Harṣa's Buddhist ideals find powerful expression in his drama *Nāgānanda*. When assured of certain and easy victory over his enemies in battle, King Jīmūtavāhana, the hero, firmly declared for the Buddhist principle of non-violence and self-sacrifice: 'Gladly, unasked, would I give my own life for another in compassion; how then could I consent to the cruel slaughter of men merely to win a realm?' [iii. 17]. In the same strain he addressed his last admonition to the cruel Garuḍa: 'Cease for ever from taking life; repent of thy past misdeeds; eagerly accumulate a store of merit, freeing all creatures from fear of thee, so that, lost in the infinite stream of thy goodness, the sin of slaying creatures, in number limited, may cease to fructify, even as a morsel of salt cast in the unfathomable depths of a great lake' [v. 25].

As a consequence of his special attentions, there was a great growth of Buddhism in Kanauj while it declined in other places. While Fa-hien could notice only two Buddhist monasteries at Kanauj, Yuan Chwang could count as many as 100 [*ibid.*].

But a true estimate of Harṣa's character must not regard him only as a Buddhist. He served other communities or the general public equally well. We have already seen how 'he regularly held the Quinquennial Convocation where he gave away in religious alms everything except the material of war' to about half a million of people of all classes and creeds! [*ibid.*] That is a record in charity and liberality which is hardly beaten in history. His daily charity amounted to the feeding of 1,000 Buddhist monks and 500 Brahmins. Yuan Chwang further informs us that 'in all the highways of the towns and villages throughout India he erected hospices (*puṇyaśālās*), provided with food and drink, and stationed there physicians with medicines for travellers and poor persons round about to be given without any stint' [Beal, i. 214]. Here also does Harṣa beat all record, perhaps even the record of Asoka, whose rest-houses for travellers did not offer them free food and medicines and medical aid! It is interesting to find that Bāṇa also furnishes similar testimony to the unique public works of utility executed under Harṣa, a testimony which brings out the cosmopolitan character of the king's public gifts: 'Beneath his rule the golden age seemed to bud forth in close-packed lines of sacrificial posts,[1] the evil time to flee in the smoke of sacrifices[1] meandering over the sky, heaven to descend in stuccoed shrines,[1] Dharma to blossom in white pennons waving over temple minarets,[1] the villages to bring forth a progeny of beautiful arbours erected on their outskirts for meetings, alms-houses, inns, and women's marquees' (133).

Along with religion, Harṣa was also noted for his pursuit and patronage of Learning. Bāṇa credits him with poetical skill and originality and wide learning: 'in poetical contests he poured out a nectar of his own which he had not received from any foreign source' (79); 'his poetical skill finds words fail'; 'his knowledge cannot find range enough in doctrines to be learned'; 'all the fine arts are too narrow a field for his genius' (86). This might be the exaggerated estimate of a courtier composing the panegyric of his patron, but we have some evidence in its support from an external source.

The Chinese traveller I-tsing who visited India after Harṣa's death (A.D. 673–87) records that King Śīlāditya was exceedingly fond of literature and at one time called for poetical compositions by the literary men of his court, whereupon it was found that they had presented their sovereign with 500 poems dealing with the popular theme of the times, the Jātakas or previous births of the Buddha. The collection of

1 Yuan Chwang mentions that 'there were more than 200 Deva-temples' in Kanauj as against 100 Buddhist monasteries [Watters, i. 340].

these poems was called *Jōtakamālā*, of which one of the authors is supposed to have been the famous Ārya Śūra [Takakusu, *I-tsing*, p. lvi]. As regards his own compositions, I-tsing says that Harṣa 'versified the story of the Bodhisattva Jīmūtavāhana (cloud-borne) who surrendered himself in place of a Nāga'. We are also told that the emperor had this play called *Nāgānanda* 'set to music and had it performed by a band accompanied by dancing and acting, and thus popularized it in his time' [ed. Takakusu, p. 163]. Historians of Sanskrit literature credit him with the authorship of two other dramas, the *Ratnāvalī* ('Necklace') and the *Priyadarśikā* (or 'Gracious Lady') together with a grammatical work. That literary criticism in ancient India thought highly of Harṣa as a poet is evident from the fact that Jayadeva, the author of *Gita-govindam*, names him along with Bhāsa and Kālidasa as one of his illustrious predecessors. Harṣa was also a skilled calligraphist if it is his autograph which is seen in the Banskhera Plate inscription, the last line of which consists of the sign-manual of the king written in elaborately ornamented characters. The emperor's sister, Rājyaśrī, also shared his intellectual tastes. 'Of great intelligence, she was distinguished for her knowledge of the Sammatīya school doctrine of Buddhism' and, 'sitting behind the king', was seen to follow with great appreciation the learned discourse of Yuan Chwang on Mahāyāna [*Life*, p. 176].

A lover and devotee of learning himself, Harṣa was

one of the best patrons of men of letters. As Bāṇa puts it, 'his learning at once suggests helping the learned' (62). Bāṇa himself, the author of *Harṣa-charita* and *Kādambarī*, was the most distinguished of his literary protégés. But we know of the names of very few who received the royal patronage in appreciation of their learning. An inscription [*Ep. Ind.* i. 180] mentions one Haridatta raised to eminence by Harṣa, while from the *Life* [p. 154] we learn that the emperor wanted to settle in his province of Orissa one of the most learned men of the times, Jayasena by name, who had become the admiration of the age by the range of his knowledge, including subjects like Hetu-vidyā, Śabdavidyā, Yoga-śāstra, the four Vedas, astronomy, geography, medicine, magic, and arithmetic, by an offer to assign to him 'the revenue of eighty large towns of Orissa'. The generosity of the donor was only beaten by the generosity of the donee, who calmly declined the repeated offer of the king on the ground that he should not trouble himself with the concerns of life or of the king! We may recall in this connexion the established maxim of Harṣa's policy that a fourth of the revenue from the crown lands should be spent on rewarding high intellectual eminence and another fourth on gifts to the various sects [Watters, i. 176].

The example of the emperor was not without its influence upon some of his subordinate kings. Kumāra, king of Assam, showed a commendable anxiety to profit by the learned company of Yuan Chwang then at Nālandā, whom he sent for by a special messenger with a letter[1] for Śīlabhadra, abbot of Nālandā, which was delivered to him after two days' journey from Assam. His request being not responded to, it was renewed through another messenger. When this also failed, 'the king with great anger sent a third messenger with a personal dispatch for Śīlabhadra, earnestly asking him to depute the Chinese pilgrim for preaching Buddhism to him and his kingdom', failing which he would 'let the evil portion of himself prevail, and, like Śaśāṅka, king of Central Bengal, who had recently destroyed the Law and uprooted the Bodhi tree, he would equip his army and elephants to raze to the ground the whole monastery of Nālandā'. This threat had the desired effect. Yuan Chwang followed his envoy to his country and stayed there for more than a month, after which King Kumāra was forced to follow him to meet Harṣa under circumstances already stated. Thenceforth Kumāra stood out as the most prominent ally of Harṣa in his support of Buddhism. At the time of parting with the Chinese pilgrim, his zeal for Buddhism showed itself in the following words addressed to him: 'If the master is able to dwell in my dominions and receive my religious offerings, I will undertake to found 100 monasteries on the master's behalf' [*Life*, pp. 170,

[1] Dr. D. B. Spooner [Arch. Sur. Report, Eastern Circle, 1917-18] discovered at Nālandā a seal of Bhāskaravarman which might have been the very seal accompanying this letter, as guessed by K. N. Dikshit [*JBORS*, 1920. p. 151].

171, 187]. We have also seen how other kings like Dhruvabhaṭṭa of Valabhī, or the kings of Jālandhara, Kashmir, and Kapis, followed Harṣa's example in supporting Buddhism.

NOTES

A. *On the Dramatic Works of Harṣa.*

The three dramas of *Ratnāvalī*, *Priyadarśikā*, and *Nāgānanda* are generally attributed to Harṣa, and this attribution rests on several grounds. In the first place, as Keith points out [*Sanskrit Drama*, 1924, p. 170], there is 'absolute similarity of style and tone in the three works which renders any effort to dissociate them wholly impossible'. The stamp of a common authorship is unmistakable throughout. The *Ratnāvalī* and the *Priyadarśikā* in special agree closely in both form and subject-matter; each is a Nāṭikā in four Acts; they have also a common hero, Udayana, and the common theme one of his numerous amourettes [*ibid.*]. All the three dramas put into the mouth of their Sūtradhāra practically the same introductory words with only the necessary modifications called for by the different titles of the Plays, and they have all in common a verse in the Prologue ascribing their authorship to Harṣa described as an accomplished poet in the same set phrases. There is, again, internal evidence to the same effect in all the dramas in the form of veiled allusions to Harṣa, and to his ideals and achievements.

The Prologue definitely mentions the assembly of kings (*rājasamūha*) from different quarters (*nānādigdeśādāgatena*) in attendance upon Śrī Harṣadeva as the king of kings[1] (*asmatsvāminā*), who had summoned them to his court on the occasion of the Spring Festival (or the Festival of Indra in *Nāgānanda*) by his rights as their paramount sovereign to which his history testifies, for it shows how he was always attended by such subordinate kings on occasions of his military adventures or religious assemblies.

But Harṣa betrays himself in his dramas in other ways. The incident introduced in the *Ratnāvalī* of the princess driven to seek shelter in the Vindhyan forest under its chief Vindhyaketu seems to have been directly suggested by the actual fact of a similar connexion which Harṣa's own sister, Princess Rājyaśrī, had with the same forest and its chiefs, Sarabhaketu and Vyāghraketu, father and son. Similarly, the following outburst of joy in which the king of his own creation in the *Ratnāvalī* indulges, Harṣa himself might indulge in under very nearly the same circumstances as are related in his actual history: 'Lo! What greater bliss can there be than this: this acquisition of an empire right up to the seas (sasāgaramahīprāpti) coupled with the recovery of the sister (bhaginīlābha)' [Act IV. 39].

There are also a few more passages where his dramas

[1] This passage alone ought to dispose of the old theory that Śrī Harṣadeva was a king of that name in Kashmir, for no king of Kashmir attained to the political status signified by the phrase, 'princes from various realms recumbent at his feet'. The ascription of these dramas to Śrī Harṣa of Kashmir (A.D. 1113-25) cannot also be maintained against the fact pointed out by Keith that 'in the *Kuṭṭanīmata* of Dāmodaragupta, who lived under Jayāpīḍa of Kashmir (A.D. 779-813), a performance of the *Ratnāvalī* ascribed to a king, is mentioned'. We may also note that citations from the *Ratnāvalī* are found in such works as *Sarasvatī Kaṇṭhābharaṇa* of Bhoja, the *Daśarūpa* of Dhanañjaya, the *Dhvanyāloka* of Ānandavardhana, which were earlier by centuries than the time of Śrī Harṣa of Kashmir.

seem to echo his history. Both the *Ratnāvalī* and the *Priyadarśikā* end with the following verse in which one finds uttered Harṣa's own hopes and aspirations as king:

'May the Lord Vāsava, sending down timely showers, make the earth yield a bumper harvest; may the best of Brahmins duly gratify the gods by their religious performances; and may there be available up to end of time the company of the Good as the source of all bliss!'

Harṣa also personally worked for the material and moral progress of his country and people.

In nearly the same strain is delivered the following by his king in the *Ratnāvalī*:

'Subdued are the enemies of the empire; on competent ministers rests the burden of administration; freed are the subjects from all kinds of trouble; and flourishing are they under peace and protection.'

Harṣa also might equally give a similar review of his own achievements.

Again, one might read a veiled allusion to Harṣa in the following verse occurring in the Prologue to the *Ratnāvalī*:

'Victorious is the king of kings (literally, the Lord of the Stars, i.e. the Moon); freed be the Brahman leaders from all troubles; productive be the earth of bounteous crops; shine the king of kings in all splendour' [Act I. 5].

Again, the descriptions of battle in both the *Ratnāvalī* and the *Priyadarśikā* (in the former between Rumaṇvat, General of Vatsarāja, and the Kośalas, in the latter between Vijayasena, General of Vatsarāja, and Vindhyaketu, the Vindhyan chief) are worthy of Harṣa as the hero of hundred battles.

'Heads were cleft by the blows of swords on helmets sore smitten; blood flowed in torrents, fire flashed from the ringing strokes; when his main host had been broken, Rumaṇvant challenged in the forefront of battle the Lord of Kośala who rode on a maddened elephant. and alone slew him with a hundred arrows.'

The king's appreciation of the heroism of his fallen foe in the *Priyadarśikā* is also worthy of a conqueror like Harṣa:

'Rumaṇvant, put to shame are we by the heroic death of Vindhyaketu who has now trod the true path of glory worthy of the most virtuous on earth: satpuruṣochitaṁ mārgamanugachchhanto yat satyaṁ vrīḍitā eva vayaṁ Vindhyaketormaraṇena.'

In the *Ratnāvalī*, too, 'there is excellent taste and propriety in Vatsa's address to the dead Kośala king: mṛityur api te ślāghyo yasya śatravo 'pyevaṁ puruṣakāraṁ varṇayanti. "Even death for thee is glorious when even thy foes must thus depict thy manly prowess." Such a phrase may reveal to us the true Harṣa himself, the winner of many victories, and the hero of one great disaster' [Keith, *op. cit.*, p. 178].

Again, the description given in the *Ratnāvalī* of the pomp and magnificence of the camp or court of Vatsa recalls Harṣa's camp as described by Bāṇa: ākṣipto jayakuñjareṇa turagān nirvarṇayan vallabhān | saṅgītadhvaninā hṛitaḥ kṣitibhṛitāṁ goṣṭhīṣu tiṣṭhan kṣaṇaṁ || The camp is described here as being marked by the incomparable stud of steeds, the elephants bringing victory, the sound of music, and the assembly of kings, just the marks of Harṣa's camp too.

The *Nāgānanda*,[1] however, evidently later than the

[1] The *Nāgānanda* seems to have been known to the poet Māgha who belonged to the eighth century A.D., and also to the poet Śivasvāmin, the court-poet of King Avantivarman of Kashmir who flourished before the end of the ninth century A.D. [Keith's *Classical Sanskrit Literature*, pp. 54, 60].

other two dramas, is conceived in a different spirit. It must have been composed in the later part of his reign when, having accomplished his conquests, he turned a Buddhist and devoted himself to the tasks of peace and religion. The plot is developed here on a different and higher plane: its main interest does not lie in the military and the violent, nor in the softer or frivolous emotions of love. The more serious and strenuous side of life, its sterner duties and more severe ideals, are brought before us. Harṣa here devotes himself to 'the task of depicting the emotions of self-sacrifice, charity, magnanimity, and resolution in the face of death' [*ibid.*]. His ideal is embodied in Jīmūtavāhana, neither a gallant, nor a military man, but a moral hero who giveth his life for others under a profound conviction that self-sacrifice is the highest duty of man, high or low. Thus his last play reflects the inner revolution wrought in Harṣa by his adoption of Buddhism on the conclusion of his conquests and campaigns. With his military spirit now crushed out of him, he who had forcibly imposed his sovereignty over all the kings of his time, the violent conqueror, and the hero of hundred battles, now takes his stand upon non-violence as the principle of his life and policy and declares himself unfit now even for a single battle: 'He who is ready to give his very life for others out of his own feeling of compassion for them, unasked and unbidden,—how can he think of the cruel slaughter of men for the sake of winning a kingdom for himself?' Thus exclaims Jīmūtavāhana against the assured prospect presented to him of the easiest victory bringing the richest result. Harṣa here speaks through him as a changed man in the later days of his life when, no longer concerned or interested in battles and conquests, he thinks only of the life spiritual, of charity and renunciation.[1]

We may now conclude by considering the allusions in later literature to Harṣa as an author. Bāṇa in the metrical introduction to his *Harṣa-charita* refers to Harṣa as Āḍhyarāja (lit. rich king) and to his achievements, literary and political (*utsāhair*). We have also two other statements of Bāṇa which definitely refer to Harsa's literary gifts: 'his gifts in poetry could hardly find expression in words' [Cowell and Thomas tr., p. 65]; Harṣa 'pouring forth in art-poesy and in stories (kāvyakathāsu) a nectar unquaffed (from other sources)' [*ibid.* p. 58]. In the *Udayasundarīkathā* [Gaekwad's Oriental Series, No. 11] of Soḍḍhala (eleventh century A.D.) is a passage which mentions Harsa along with Vikramāditya

[1] It may be noted that various other theories have been advanced even from olden times on the authorship of these dramas. We have already disposed of the theory which fathers them on Śrī Harṣa of Kashmir. But the oldest theory is that of Mammaṭa, who in his *Kāvyaprakāśa* speaks of Harṣa's gift of gold to Bāṇa (or Dhāvaka in some MSS.), and the commentators connect this gift with the *Ratnāvalī* which was passed off in Harṣa's name by his own court poet. But it is difficult to believe in Bāṇa's authorship of these dramas, considering how very disparate are the styles of these dramas and the *Harṣa-charita*, as rightly pointed out by Keith. There is again a passage in Rājaśekhara's *Kāvyamīmāṁsā* where these dramas are named in the order of their composition (*Priyadarśikā* being named as the earliest and *Nāgānanda* the last) and ascribed to Dhāvaka Bhāsa, who from a poor washerman came to be the prince of poets (Dhāvako'pi hi yad Bhāsaḥ kavīnāmagrimobhavat) and was made his court poet by King Śrī Harṣa-Vikrama. Perhaps this passage was the source of Mammaṭa's statement—'Śrī Harṣāder Dhāvakādīnamiva dhanam', of which an alternate reading was 'Śrī Harṣāder Bāṇādīnamiva dhanam', as pointed out above. The truth of the whole matter is that either Harṣa composed the dramas himself or permitted their unknown author to compose them in his name.

[probably Chandragupta II], Muñja, and Bhoja, as being both *bhūpāla* and *kavīndra*, king and prince of poets, who presided over a literary court (*sabhā*). Another passage in the same work punningly refers to Harṣa as one 'whose joy (harṣa) lay in words (gīrharṣa) in his own assembly (nijasaṃsadi), and who, as king, had honoured Bāṇa with an offering of a hundred crors of gold' (sampūjitaḥ kanakakoṭiśatena Bāṇaḥ). The famous poet, Jayadeva [who cannot be placed later than the eleventh century A.D. according to Sten Konow (*Das indische drama*, pp. 87–8), and some of whose stanzas are cited in Sārṅgadhara's Paddhati (A.D. 1363)], mentions Harṣa along with Bhāsa and Kālidāsa, his contemporaries, Bāṇa and Mayūra, and the later Chora, as authors of equal rank. Similarly, Madhusūdana, writing about A.D. 1654, associates Bāṇa and Mayūra with Harṣa's court and speaks of Harṣa as 'the chief of the race of poets (Kavijanamūrdhanyasya), the author of the Nāṭikā called *Ratnāvalī*, the lord of Mālava and its capital Ujjayinī'.

Again, besides the three dramas, there are a few other compositions traceable to Harṣa's authorship. The inscriptions on both the Banskhera and Madhuban plates, of which the former is attested by Harṣa's own signature, are evidently his own composition. They contain metrical stanzas which represent some fine poetry. One of these (Bans. 5–6 = Madh. 6–7) in the Śārdūlavikrīḍitā metre refers with the warmth of a personal feeling to the death by treachery of his elder brother, Rājyavardhana. A second (B. 13 = M. 16) in the Vasantatilaka metre, describing Fortune as unstable, like lightning or a bubble of water, urges upon his family and others the faithful performance of the royal donative decree. Then follows the beautiful verse:

'By body, mind, and speech should good be done to

all creatures: this has been declared by Harṣa as the best acquisition of Dharma or religious merit.'

There are, lastly, two short Sanskrit poems of Buddhistic content which are also attributed to Harṣa. One of these called the Suprabhātastotra, a matin hymn in praise of the Buddha, mentions Harṣa's name in the colophon [Dr. F. W. Thomas in *JRAS*, 1903, p. 703–22], while the other, entitled Aṣṭamahāśrīchaityasaṁskṛitastotra, a hymn to the Eight Great Buddhist Shrines, preserved in Chinese, is attributed by Yuan Chwang to an Indian king designated in Chinese as 'Sun of Virtue' = Śīlāditya, the title by which Harṣa was known [Nariman, Jackson, and Ogden's *Priyadarśikā*, p. xlv, Columbia University Publication, to which I owe some of the references and suggestions utilized in this Note].

B. *The Art of the Gupta Age.*

In connexion with the history of India under Harṣa, it may not be amiss to consider the condition of Indian art in that age. In the time of Harṣa what is known as *Gupta Art* had attained its full fruition and fruitage, although it is difficult to determine definitely which of its numerous and noted examples connect themselves with the reign of Harṣa. A brief survey is therefore given here of the main characteristics of Gupta art as a whole with reference to the best examples known of each.

The Gupta period was the golden age not merely of Indian literature but also of Indian art. The renaissance was the result of the self-expression which India was enabled to achieve as a politically organized unit under the paramount authority exercised for several centuries by a succession of brilliant Gupta emperors. Thus with a new sense of self-realization, India was even making herself felt among her neighbours. Her thought invaded the countries of the Far East by way of Central Asia, and Further India and Indonesia by sea, her relations with the east following the period of her relations with the west, by way of Bactria in the north, and of the Roman trade in the south, under the Kuṣāṇas and the Andhras.

The true spirit of Indian culture, its catholicity, and comprehensiveness, were represented in the Gupta emperors who, instead of making either Brahminism or Buddhism as the state religion, patronized equally the leading creeds of the times, their offshoots. These were Vaiṣṇavism, Śaivism, Śāktism, and Mahāyāna Buddhism, centring respectively round Viṣṇu, Śiva, Devī, Buddha, or Bodhisattva. Images and temples connected with these creeds mark the artistic history of the period.

We may now briefly refer to the most important of the extant examples of each of these classes. The brick temple of Bhitargāon in the Cawnpore district assigned to the sixth century A.D., square in plan with a high tower, is decorated with carved brickwork and brilliant terra-cotta panels illustrating Śaiva themes. Near Besnagar in Gwalior are cave temples in the Udayagiri hills, one of which bears an inscription of A.D. 401, where we find vigorous sculptures representing the incarnation of Viṣṇu as Varāha and also the goddesses Gaṅgā and Yamunā standing on the Makara. At Pathāri in the same neighbourhood there is a massive relief on the nativity of Kṛiṣṇa showing the new-born babe lying by the side of the mother watched by five attendants. Beglar considered this as the finest and largest piece of Indian sculpture.

The temple at Deogarh in the Lalitpur subdivision of the Jhansi district assigned to the sixth century A.D. has sculptures of exceptionally good quality in panels. One of these representing Śiva as a Yogī may, according to V. Smith, claim a place among the best effoıts of Indian culture. Another panel represents Viṣṇu reclining on Ananta, the serpent, the symbol of eternity. Beautiful Kṛiṣṇa scenes including the raising of Mount Govardhana are also depicted in fragmentary sculptures of the fourth century A.D. found at Mandor near Jodhpur. In Kosam in the Allahabad district was found a remarkable group in sculpture of Śiva and Pārvatī with an inscription dated A.D. 458.

We may next note the Durgā temple at Aihole showing the dancing Śiva type of the fifth century and a few other temples of the sixth century showing Vaiṣṇava reliefs which are closely related to the excavated architectural forms of the neighbouring Bādāmi caves considered to be the finest Hindu sculptures by Havell and Coomārswāmi. Cave I is a Śaiva temple with a Tāṇḍava sculptured relief. Caves II and III are Vaiṣṇava temples. Cave IV is a Jaina cave with relief sculptures of the Jinas. Elura was another noted centre of Gupta Brahminical art. There is a Daśāvatāra or Ten Incarnations cave of about A.D. 700, including the Bhairava and Kālī group, and the rescue of Mārkaṇḍeya by Śiva. There is also a Kailāsa temple at Elura of slightly later date, showing a beautiful Tāṇḍava.

But Gupta art is perhaps seen at its best in its Buddhist branch. Some of the earlier examples are the sculptures of Garhwa near Allahabad, bearing inscriptions assignable to Chandragupta II, Kumargupta I, and Skandagupta, but the best examples are found at Sārnāth. Though the sculptures discovered at Sārnāth belong to different periods, the great majority of them belong to Gupta times. We find in them clear proofs of emancipation of the indigenous art from the foreign influences. The Buddha image of the period, for instance, though descended from the Kushāṇa image, exhibits 'a new and purely national development and indeed represents a new type which in artistic merit is infinitely superior to its predecessor. Some of the Buddha statues of this period, by their wonderful expression of calm repose and mild serenity, give a beautiful rendering of the Buddhist ideal. The indications of the drapery having been almost wholly discarded, the monastic robes are merely marked in outline. On the contrary, the halo encircling the head of the Master becomes lavishly ornamented with floral and foliated ornament. Evidently the real significance of this "Circle of Light" (prabhāmaṇḍala) was completely forgotten. The Gupta sculptors thus went far to eliminate or modify those features which in the Kushāṇa period still indicated the foreign origin of the Buddha image' [Dr. Vogel in *Sārnāth Museum Catalogue*, p. 19].

The seated Buddha-image, showing him preaching his first sermon at Isipatana, is regarded as one of the masterpieces of Indian art, with its symbolism further developed in the position of the hands (known as Dharma-Chakra-Mudrā), and in the wheel and the two deer carved on the pedestal to indicate the Wheel of the Law and the Deer Park where the Wheel was first turned.

In the Gupta period were also developed what are called the Mudrās which play such a prominent part in later Buddhist iconography.

We also see in these Buddha sculptures a more critical sense of the importance of the principal figure of the Buddha, as compared with other figures which, though associated with him in life, are now much reduced in size and subordinated in position.

While early Buddhist art avoided figuring the Buddha on principle, the Gupta art fashioned his figure in large numbers and a variety of forms. Images of the Master were installed in the monasteries, in their cells, special chapels, and temples, and even in their outer niches and relic towers.

Another marked feature of the Gupta sculptures is their domination by the cult of the Bodhisattvas which is now very pronounced. We have many an image not merely of Maitreya, but also, and in particular, of Avalokiteśvara.

We also note a further development in the history of Buddhism by the introduction of the images of numerous other deities borrowed from the Brahminical pantheon, such as Vaiśravana, god of wealth, the goddess of fertility, Vasudhārā, the goddess of plenty, Tārā, Mārīchī, &c., of which the Sārnāth excavations have yielded so many specimens.

With the expansion of the Buddhist pantheon and multiplication of divine images, there is noticed a decreasing tendency to produce sculptures directly bearing on the life of the Buddha. In this respect the Gupta art separates itself from the Graeco-Buddhist art of Gandhara, which was at such pains to produce myriads of sculptures illustrative of every possible incident in the life of the Buddha. For the same reason, we find that the Jātakas no longer inspire the art of the period to the extent to which they have the earliest art.

Besides Sārnāth, some of the best examples of the Gupta sculptures are being brought to light at Nālandā, as the result of the excavations there.

Besides sculptures, the progress of the Gupta art is

also exhibited in the seals and gold coins of the period, which are masterpieces of design.

In the British Museum is also preserved a small gold standing image of the Buddha of this period. A reference may also be made to the iron pillar of Delhi supposed to have been erected about the fifth century A.D. by King Chandra Varmā, one of the kings of Āryāvarta, conquered by Samudragupta.

Lastly, some of the best examples of both sculpture and painting for the period are seen at Ajantā. The caves there are twenty-nine in number and range in date from about A.D. 50–642. No. XIII may even date from 200 B.C., as its figures are akin to those of Sāñchi. Nos. VIII–XIII are assigned to 200 B.C.–150 A.D., as they are concerned with Hīnayāna Buddhism. Nos. VI and VII were between A.D. 450–550. Nos. I–V, XIV–XXIX are believed to have been excavated between A.D. 500–642.

It may also be noted that Nos. IX, X, XIX, and XXVI are in the form of Chaityas or churches, while the rest are like Vihāras.

Among the Ajantā sculptures may be noted:

(1) The Buddha with attendants on the gateway of Cave IX.

(2) River goddesses on the entrances of Caves XVI and XXII.

(3) The dying Buddha, 23¼ ft. in length, in Cave XXVI.

(4) The temptation of the Buddha in the same cave.

(5) Incidents in the lives of the Buddha figured in Cave I.

The paintings are too well known to be noticed here. They call for a special treatment.

CHAPTER VI

Economic Conditions

From the moral we now proceed to consider the material progress of the country as described by Yuan Chwang. The centres of prosperity were the cities, of which some new ones sprang into importance in the India under Harṣa, while some of the older and historically important cities were on the wane, as the main currents of life in the country flowed away from them along new courses. Pāṭaliputra was no longer the premier city of Northern India. Its place was taken by Kanauj on the Ganges, a cosmopolitan city where both Buddhism and Brahminism were flourishing with 100 monasteries accommodating 10,000 monks and 200 Deva-temples. The city, about five miles in length and a mile and a half in breadth, was very strongly defended. Its prosperity was expressed in its 'lofty structures, beautiful gardens, tanks of clear water, and the museum of rarities collected from strange lands'. It was equally manifest in 'the refined appearance of its citizens, their clothes of glossy silk, their devotion to learning and arts, their clear and suggestive discourses, and the number of the well-to-do classes and families with great wealth' [Watters, i. 340]. It was in every way a fit place for the great assembly held by Harṣa. Prayāga or Allahabad had also become an important place with the revival of Brahminism with which it is associated, and claimed to be the seat of the most important of Harṣa's institutions, his Quinquennial Convocation of Mokṣa, where the people from all parts of India gathered in their lacs for his charities. The decline of Buddhism meant that of its holy cities. Śrāvastī, where even Fa-hien saw ninety-eight monasteries, was now seen as a mass of ruins by Yuan Chwang who found only one monastery there. Kapilavastu, the Bethlehem of Buddhism, which once boasted of more than 1,000 monasteries, now had only one with thirty monks! In the Vaiśāli country, another great stronghold of Buddhism, 'it must have been distressing for our pilgrim to go over the waste jungle-covered ruins of a district which he had known from the Buddhist scriptures to have been once very flourishing' [Watters, ii. 77]. Buddhism was, however, reviving in a few new centres like Nālandā in Eastern India and Valabhī in Western India, which were now at the height of their glory. The other flourishing cities of India under Harṣa which Yuan Chwang did not omit to visit or to describe were *Mathurā*, twenty *li* or four miles in circuit, famous for 'its fine striped cotton cloth and gold', its temples and vihāras, its stūpas built by Asoka, and those for the relics of the Buddha's chief disciples [Watters, i. 301–2]; *Sthāneśvara*, with its 100 temples, and prosperous trade bringing the rarities of other lands [*ibid.*, p. 314], originally the capital of Harṣa; *Matipura*, near Bijnor, with its 50 temples, its grain, fruit, and flowers [*ibid.*, p. 322]; *Mayūra* or Hardwar, with its large population, and drawing, besides, 'constantly many thousands of people from distant regions for bathing in its sacred waters, its many *puṇyaśālās* endowed by pious kings for free distribution, among the needy, of dainty food and medical requisites [*ibid.*, p. 328]; *Goviśana* (modern Rāmpur and Pilibhit), with a flourishing population and 30 temples; *Ahichchhatra* and *Pi-lo-shan-na*; *Kapitha* or Sankāśra; *Ayodhyā* with 100 Buddhist vihāras and 10 temples; *Kośāmbi*, near Śrāvasti and north of Prayāga, according to Watters, with its 50 temples, but Buddhism in decay; *Viśoka* (in the Barabanki district, according to Vincent Smith), with its 20 Buddhist monasteries and 50 temples; *Vārāṇasī*, with its more than 100 temples 'with storeyed terraces and temple-eaves of carved stone and wood', its 'city-wards close together, its very numerous inhabitants having boundless wealth, with their houses full of rare valuables'; *Champā* and *Rājamahal* in Bihar; *Puṇyavardhana* (Rangpur) in Bengal, with its 100 temples, 20 vihāras, flourishing population, and 'tanks, hospices, and flowery groves alternating here and there'; *Sumataṭa* (Faridpur in Bengal), which had more than 30 vihāras and 100 temples; *Tāmralipti*, with more than 50 temples, the port of Bengal for voyages; *Karṇasuvarṇa* (identified with Burdwan, Birbhum, and Murshidabad districts, the territory of Śaśāṅka), of which the capital (unidentified) was above four miles in circuit; and, lastly, *Kāmarūpa*, with hundreds of temples, under King Kumāra, Harṣa's ally.

The architecture of the cities and the methods of town-planning adopted point to the high degree of economic progress achieved. Architects are called *Gṛihachintakas* by Bāṇa. The cities were enclosed within quadrangular walls, broad and high. The walls were generally built of bricks, while the walls of houses and enclosures were wattled bamboo or wood, where the country was low and moist. The high-class houses had 'their halls and terraced belvederes which had wooden flat-roofed rooms, were coated with chunam, and covered with tiles burnt or unburnt'. They were also of great height. As regards whitewashing, Bāṇa describes how 'workmen mounted on ladders, with brushes upheld in their hands and plaster pails on their shoulders, whitened the top of the street wall of the palace' (158). The houses of the poor, 'thatched with coarse or common grass, were of brick or boards; their walls were ornamented with chunam, and the floor purified with cow-dung and strewn with flowers of the season'. Yuan Chwang considered the architecture of the public buildings, the Buddhist monasteries, to be 'most remarkable'. 'They have a tower at each of the four corners of the quadrangle and three high halls in a tier. The rafters and roof-beams are carved with strange figures, and the doors, windows, and walls are painted in various colours'.[1] But the private houses had 'a sumptuous inside but a simple outside'.

Among the furniture are mentioned seats which were corded benches. These were variously adorned according as they were used by the royal family, the grandees, officials, and the gentry. The frames of the seats were carved in different ways according to different tastes. The sovereign sat on a dais, very wide and high, and dotted with small pearls. On the dais was placed his actual throne, the 'Lion's Seat', as Yuan Chwang translates it, which was covered with fine cloth and mounted by a jewelled footstool. We have already seen that Bāṇa also, like Yuan Chwang, noticed Harṣa using a jewelled footstool.

Yuan Chwang mentions some details about town-planning too. The thoroughfares appeared to him as narrow, tortuous passages, but in other respects the town-planning followed certain principles. Shops were placed on the highways, and the booths or inns on the roads. Persons following unclean or disreputable occupations had to live outside the city. These

[1] We may refer in this connexion to the buildings and architecture of the Nālandā monastery as described by Yuan Chwang. He speaks of its storeyed buildings, richly adorned towers, upper rooms and turrets towering above the clouds. The massive external grandeur of the buildings contrasted with the delicate beauty of their interior, with 'the dragon-projections, coloured eaves, pearl-red pillars carved and ornamented, richly adorned balustrades, and roofs covered with shining tiles reflecting light in a thousand shades', while 'the sculpture was perfect' [*Life*, p 111, and Watters, ii. 165].

were butchers, fishermen, public performers executioners, and scavengers. Their houses were also marked out by distinguishing signs. They would, when working within the city, sneak along on the left, as they went about in the houses. These regulations were laid down in the interests of the physical and moral well-being of the citizens, as provided for in the Brahminical law-books.

Besides architecture, sculpture, and the building industry, much progress was shown in manufactures. Yuan Chwang mentions various kinds of cloth then used. First, there were the *Kauṣeya* cloths made of silk and cotton. Secondly, there was the *Kṣauma* or linen cloth made of fabrics derived from the stuffs from the three plants, the flax, the jute, and the hemp. The third variety of wearing material was the *Kambala*, woollen cloth or blanket. The fourth class of cloth was that made of the wool of a wild animal, which was very fine, soft, and easily spun and woven. The people, however, used very simple dress comprising inner clothing and outward attire, which did not involve any tailoring work. 'The men wind a strip of cloth round the waist and up to the armpits and leave the shoulder bare. The women wear a long robe which covers both shoulders and falls down loose.' Close-fitting jackets were used in parts of Northern India in winter where the cold was severe. The Chinese pilgrim was glad to accept the gift of a fur-lined cape from the king of Assam as a protection against cold. Ornaments were freely used by the kings and grandees. Garlands and bejewelled tiaras were used for the head, and rings, bracelets, and necklaces for the body. Wealthy merchants used only bracelets.

Industrial life was organized on the basis of castes, and larger corporations or guilds. The Brahmins had no part in the industrial life of the country, but lived as non-economic men concerned only with the spiritual interests of life. The work of administration was taken over by the Kṣatriyas. Trade, inland and foreign, was in the hands of the Vaiśyas. Agriculture, the main industry of the country, was in the hands of the Śūdras. As means of irrigation, Bāṇa refers to what he calls *tulāyantra* or water-pump. Yuan Chwang also refers to the 'mixed castes', i. e., corporations admitting of a heterogenous composition, and hence guilds (as explained by Watters) which were numerous in the country [Watters, i. 147, 148, 168]. Bāṇa (158) describes how on the occasion of Princess Rājyaśrī's marriage, 'from every country were summoned guilds of skilled artists' to decorate the palace, such as carpenters, painters, modellers, and the like. He also refers to the system of apprenticeship, the apprentices being called *navasevakas*.

An idea of the variety and excellence of the manufactures of the times may be gained from a study of the royal presents as described by Bāṇa and the Chinese pilgrim. The presents sent by the king of Assam to Harṣa included an exquisitely-ornamented umbrella with jewelled ribs and the external wrapper of white bark-silk: crest jewels; pearl necklaces; silken towels rolled up in baskets of variously coloured reeds; quantities of pearl, shell, sapphire, and other drinking vessels embossed by skilful artists; leather bucklers with charming borders and gold-leaf work winding about them: soft loin-cloths; pillows of deer's leather and other figured textures; cane stools; volumes of fine writing with leaves made from aloe bark; carved boxes, and so forth (243). Yuan Chwang also refers to the full-size statue of the Buddha in gold made for worship at the Assembly of Kanauj, to which the king also presented as an offering 'a golden dish, a golden cup, seven golden ewers, one golden staff, 3,000 gold pieces or coins, and 3,000 vestments of superior cotton-stuff' [*Life*, p. 178]. Yuan Chwang himself carried away from India, among other things, books and manuscripts, images of the Buddha in gold, silver, and sandal-wood. He also says that 'gold, silver, white jade, and crystal lenses were very abundant in India' [Watters, i. 178].

Lastly, we may note that the money or the medium of exchange in India in those days comprised, according to the account of the Chinese pilgrim, not merely the gold and silver coins, but also cowries and small pearls [*ibid.*].

CHAPTER VII

SOCIAL LIFE.

IT remains now to consider the social life, the manners and customs of the people in that age. Society was based on caste and governed by its rules. Besides the four castes, Yuan Chwang also mentions the 'mixed castes'. 'The four castes form classes of various degrees of ceremonial purity.' The Kṣatriyas and Brahmins are described by Yuan Chwang to be 'clean-handed, and unostentatious, pure and simple in life, and very frugal'. He also says: 'among the various castes and classes of the country the Brahmins were purest and in most esteem', and they gave their name to the country: 'the name Brāhmaṇa-country had come to be a popular one for India.' There were no inter-caste marriages. 'Relations whether by the father's or the mother's side do not intermarry,' says Yuan Chwang.

The restrictions of caste as regards food and marriage were not, however, allowed to interfere with the free social intercourse between different castes in other respects. Bāṇa, for instance, came of an orthodox and learned Brahmin family, and yet the circle of his most intimate associates and dearest comrades included two *Pāraśava* brothers (who are first mentioned), two

Vandinas (bards), one *Kātyāyanikā* (ascetic widow without any caste), one *Jāṅgalika* (snake doctor), a betel-bearer, a goldsmith (*Kalāda*), a supervisor (*Hairika*), a scribe (*Lekhaka*), a painter (*Chitrakṛit*), a *Pustakakṛit* (notary), a drummer (*Mārdaṅgika*), two musicians, one *Sairandhrī* (maid), two pipers (*Vāṁśika*), a music-master, a shampooer (*Saṁvāhika*), a dancer (*Lāsaka*), a dicer (*Akṣika*), a gamester (*Kitava*), an actor (*Śailāli*), a dancing-girl (*Nartakī*), a Pārāśara ascetic, a Digambara Jaina (*Kṣapaṇaka*), a Śaiva ascetic, a metallurgist (*Dhātuvādavid*), a potter (*Dārdurika*), and a juggler (*Aindrajālika*). We have thus evidence here not merely of free intercourse between different castes and crafts, but also between different sexes. Life in that age even for the strict and orthodox Brahmin was quite merry and free!

Yuan Chwang noticed the physical purity of the people. 'They are pure of themselves and not from compulsion. Before every meal they must have a wash; the fragments and remains are not served up again; the food utensils are not passed on; the utensils that are of pottery or wood must be thrown away after use, but the metallic ones, those made of gold, silver, copper, or iron were used after cleansing.' Like Fa-hien, Yuan Chwang also observed the purity of diet used by the Indians. 'Onions and garlic are little used, and people who eat them are ostracized.' Meat was forbidden, except mutton and venison. Fish was also allowed, but the common food comprised milk, ghee, granulated sugar, sugar-candy, cakes, and parched grain with mustard oil [Watters, i. 140, 151, 152, 168, and 178].

The life at the court and of the upper classes does not seem to have been so pure and puritanical, if we may believe in the behaviour of the palace on the occasion of the festivities in celebration of the birth of Harṣa, as described by Bāṇa. The scene was one of unbridled mirth and licence to which contributed the 'drunken slave women alluring the favourites, old feudatories clasping in a dance the intoxicated bawds, naughty slave-boys betraying in songs the secret amours of the ministers of state, other slaves carrying on a war of foul language, king's women, frolicky young men, and harlot-women'. 'All womenkind being set dancing, even old ladies shouted like maniacs. Old men even lost all shame, as though bewitched. The wise forgot themselves, as if intoxicated. Even hermits' hearts were all agog for a dance' (144 f.). In the *Ratnāvalī*, too, Harṣa gives a picture of the merriment and licence to which the citizens of towns abandoned themselves on the occasion of the spring festival. We read of drunken and dancing women, besmeared with vermilion, and bathed in water from syringes shaped like hoods of serpents, embracing their friends decked in their best garments, while the openings of highways resounded with their clappings. We also read of theatres (*Prekṣāgṛiha*) musical saloons, and picture-galleries where the citizens enjoyed themselves. All this is no doubt a poet's exaggeration, but even the exaggeration is based on a substratum of truth. All that we may guess is that these features of court and city life had perhaps disappeared under the later austere régime of Harṣa when he turned a Buddhist and 'assumed the red garments together with his sister' (289), just as many customs and practices of his predecessors ceased to be under Asoka.

We have some evidence indicating the status of women in those days. The women of higher classes went in for education, and did not live in complete seclusion. Princess Rājyaśrī, as we have seen, was educated enough to follow the learned discourse of Yuan Chwang on Mahāyāna, while Bāṇa tells us how her royal brother had engaged the famous Buddhist sage Divākaramitra to discourse to her on Buddhist doctrines (289). Admission to the royal harem does not seem to have been very strict. According to a passage in Bāṇa's *Kādambarī*, it freely included aged ascetic women of different sects, 'followers of the Arhat, Kṛiṣṇa, Viśravasa, Avalokiteśvara, and Viriñcha', so as to make it quite catholic in its religious outlook and sympathies! There were also arrangements in the palace for training the princesses in the fine arts and accomplishments. Rājyaśrī, according to Bāṇa, was trained up in song and dance by experts retained for the purpose. In Harṣa's own drama of *Priyadarśikā*, the king assigns to the queen the task of arranging for the instruction of the maid, Priyadarśikā, in dancing, vocal and instrumental music (gītanṛityavādyādiṣu). One of the accomplishments of these ladies seems to have been painting. The *Ratnāvalī* represents the heroine drawing the portrait of her lover on the picture-board (*chitraphalaka*) with brush (*vartikā*) and colours carried in a basket (*samudgaka*). There are also references in these dramas to the Schools for Painting and Music (*Chitraśālā* and *Gandharvaśālā*). We may also note that early marriages of women were the order of the day. Princess Rājyaśrī was married before she had attained puberty. She also became widowed very early in her life, and remained a widow throughout. As Yuan Chwang informs us, 'a woman never contracts a second marriage'. That Rājyaśrī did not observe *purdah* is also evident from the fact that she 'was sitting behind the king' as she heard the discourse of the Chinese pilgrim [*Life*, p. 176], and also from her freedom of movements among the Vindhyan jungles under circumstances already stated. We may also note that the custom of *Satī* or the voluntary self-immolation of widows on the funeral pyres of their husbands was then known. Princess Rājyaśrī was herself following her husband unto death till she was stopped at the last moment by her brother's very timely intervention. Queen Yaśovatī was the best example of a Satī as described by Bāṇa (187): against the fervent protests of her worthy son, Harṣa, she resolved she 'would die while still unwidowed', and declared in her devotion to her dying husband: 'Not to die, but to live at such a time would be unfeeling. Compared with the flame of wifely sorrow, whose fuel is imperishable love, fire itself is chilly cold'. Then, having embraced her son and kissed his head, the queen, a queen over Death itself, went forth on foot from the women's quarter and in the midst of the citizens' lamentations proceeded straight to the banks of the Sarasvatī where, after worshipping the fire, she plunged into it, 'to go before, like the dust of her husband's feet, to announce his coming to the heavens'! In his *Priyadarśikā*, Harṣa describes the case of a Satī, of the wife of Vindhyaketu following him to death. Inscription No. 20 of Fleet of A.D. 510 commemorates how the wife of the chief Goparāja who fell fighting for his Gupta overlord, Bhānugupta, died as a Satī. Such examples of wifely chastity and devotion in high places, in royal households, could not but purify and elevate the general moral atmosphere of the country.

Sea voyages were common.[1] We read of a Brahmin envoy sent by Harṣa to China in A.D. 641. When Yuan Chwang was about to begin his return journey to China, Harṣa inquired by what route he proposed to return, and said to him: 'If you select the southern sea-route, then I will send official attendants to accompany you' [*Life*, p. 188], thereby implying that Harṣa's administration was more familiar with the sea-route to China, along which travelled the many

[1] The *Ratnāvalī* tells of the sea-voyage of its heroine from Ceylon to Kauśāmbī, of the shipwreck on the way, and of her rescue from a plank on which she was floating by a sea-trader of Kauśāmbī (*samudreyānabhaṅgaṇımagnāyāḥ phālakāsādananam*).

embassies, merchants, missionaries, and pilgrims who had helped during several centuries to bring the two countries closer in bonds of political, commercial, and cultural intercourse. This was the route taken, for instance, by Fa-hien in the fourth century A. D. both for his outward and return journey. From Tāmralipti, the port of embarkation in India, Fa-hien reached Ceylon by a voyage of fourteen days. Thence he came to Java, the next halting-place, in a big vessel carrying more than 200 passengers. From Java, a similar vessel carried him to Kwang-Chow in fifty days, since the boat carried provisions for its passengers to last for that period. The passengers, more than 200 in number, were all 'Brahmins', i.e., followers of Brahminism, and were all traders. But this sea-borne trade of India and her colonizing and missionary activities showed an increase during the spacious times of the Gupta emperors, and of Harṣa. The Javanese Chronicles refer to a great emigration of about 5,000 Indians (including cultivators, artisans, warriors, physicians, and writers, i.e., the classes of workers who can build up a self-contained colony) from the west coast of India to Java about A D. 603 in six large and 100 small vessels, followed by another contingent of 2,000 emigrants who were carvers in stone and brass. To these craftsmen from India we owe the great temples of Borobudur and Prambanam in Java which are some of the best examples of Indian art. It is inferred that these immigrants from the Gujarat ports might be the Śakas, whose power had collapsed under the conquests of Chandragupta II, and also the white Huns whose defeat by the Sassanians and Turks between A.D. 550–600 intercepted their retreat northwards. Then there were also the conquests of Prabhākaravardhana who had defeated the Huns, the Gurjaras, the Lātas, and the kings of Gandhāra, Sindh, and Malwa, followed by the further conquests of Harṣa himself, driving swarms of refugees towards the Gujarat ports, anxious to escape from a land of disturbance and confusion into fresh fields and pastures new. Thus these large movements and migrations opened up more fully the sea-routes to the farther east, the approaches to new fields of commerce and colonization. In the itinerary of I-tsing, who came to India shortly after Harṣa's death, we notice how thoroughly these were explored and exploited. I-tsing set sail from China in a Persian ship in A.D. 671. Before sailing twenty days, the ship reached the first station named Bhoja, the capital of the country called Śrībhoja. From there I-tsing embarked in another ship, and, after fifteen days' sail, reached Malayu, then a part of Śrībhoja. Thence he set sail in another ship and came to Ka-cha, a port of Śrībhoja, after another fifteen days. Then in another ship belonging to the king of this country, he arrived after ten days' sail at what was known as 'the country of the naked people' (probably the Nicobar Islands) whence, in a direct voyage towards India for about a fortnight, he disembarked at the great port of Tāmralipti. I-tsing gives the following further particulars for the return voyage: 'Sailing from Tāmralipti two months in the south-east direction, we come to Ka-cha. By this time, a ship from Bhoja will have arrived there. But those who go to Ceylon must sail in south-west direction. We stay in Ka-cha till winter, thence start on board ship for the south, and we come after a month to the country of Malayu or Bhoja. We stay there till the middle of summer and we sail to the north. In about a month we reach Kwang-fu. I have thus shortly described the route and the way home, hoping that the wise will still expand their knowledge by hearing more' [see Takakusu's ed., Introd.].

These facilities of shipping and navigation were called for by the needs of commercial as well as cultural intercourse between the countries concerned. There was a brisk export of both goods and ideas from India to these distant countries beyond her borders, which figure as so many outposts of Indian culture in the record of I-tsing. The chief of these was the island of Sumatra, then known as Malayu or Śrībhoja, a colony of Java, itself the stronghold of Indian influence. I-tsing studied here both Sanskrit and Pali for years. In the capital he found more than 1,000 monks who studied all the subjects that were studied in the most cultured part of India, the Madhyadeśa Java, called Javadi by Fa-hien (A.D. 414), is called Kaliṅga in I-tsing's time. Brahmmism was first established there, and then Buddhism. A Sumatra inscription of A.D. 656 names King Ādityadharma as the ruler of Java, while Sanskrit and Vaiṣṇava inscriptions are found there, dating from the fifth century. I-tsing's general observation is that 'many kings and chieftains in the islands of the Southern Ocean (of which he enumerates more than eleven) admire and believe Buddhism'; they are 'all under the influence of Buddhism' [*ibid.*].[1]

Indeed, the age of Harṣa witnessed a considerable development of a Greater India beyond the limits of India both towards the islands of the southern seas and the eastern countries. Indian culture was spreading in all the neighbouring countries of India. Some of the best evidence of this for the time of Harṣa is given also by the Chinese pilgrim, Yuan Chwang. On his way from China to India and back by the land-route, he noticed decisive marks of Indian influence in many of the countries he had to pass through. In the country of *Yenki* he found 'above ten Buddhist monasteries with above 2,000 ecclesiastics of the Sar-

[1] The subject of Indian influence in these foreign countries demands a volume by itself. Perhaps the best recent account is given in Eliot's monumental work, *Hinduism and Buddhism*, in three volumes. We may cite in this connexion the evidence of some inscriptions discovered. In the Wellesley district of the Mālaya Peninsula has been found an inscription of the fourth century A.D. of a Buddhist naval captain (mahānāvika) named Buddhagupta hailing from Raktamṛttikā (= Rāṅgāmāṭi of Murshidabad district, Bengal). Several Śaiva Hindu kings tracing their descent to Aśvatthāmā, son of Droṇa, are mentioned as kings in Further India from the second to the seventh century A.D. in a series of inscriptions. An inscription of the fifth century A.D. in Pallava characters found at Koetei in East Borneo mentions King Mūlavarman ruling there [see *IA*, 1921, p. 117].

vāstivādin school of Hīnayāna. Since as to the sūtra teaching and Vinaya regulations they followed India, it is in its literature that students of these subjects study them thoroughly'. We are further told that, besides literature, the very writing of this country is 'taken from that of India with slight modification' [Watters, i. 48 f.]. Watters also informs us from Chinese sources that this country had the famous monastery known as Araṇya-vihāra where the great Indian sage, Dharmagupta, had lodged in the year A.D. 585 when on his way to China. Next, in the country of *Ku-chih*, the traveller noticed more than 100 Buddhist monasteries with above 5,000 brethren of the same Sarvāstivādin school studied in the language and works of India, which also gave to this country its writing, though much altered [*ibid.*, p. 59]. Watters informs us from other Chinese sources that the number of Buddhist buildings and images throughout this land was very great. We are also told of two monasteries in the neighbourhood, Eastern and Western, with images of the Buddha 'beautiful almost beyond human skill', while the former had a slab of jade-stone bearing an impress of the Buddha's foot. Outside the city of *Ku-chih*, 'there were two standing images of the Buddha above 90 ft. high which marked the place where the great quinquennial Buddhist assemblies were held, and at which the annual autumn religious meetings of clergy and laity occurred. The latter meetings lasted for some tens of days and were attended by ecclesiastics from all parts of the country. While these convocations were sitting the king and all his subjects made holiday, abstaining from work, keeping fast, and hearing religious discourses. All the monasteries made processions with their images of the Buddha borne on vehicles'. Thus we find in this distant country established some of the chief Buddhist institutions of India, including the assemblies which Harṣa himself used to celebrate with such pomp and magnificence. Close by was a very famous monastery known as *Āścharya Vihāra*, 'with spacious halls and artistic images of the Buddha and a place of resort for men of eminence from distant lands, who were hospitably entertained by the king and officials and people.' From the *Life* we learn that the host of Yuan Chwang in this monastery was Mokṣagupta, a Hīnayānist who had studied above twenty years in India and was known for his knowledge of the commentaries and etymology. But even he yielded to Yuan Chwang in learning and became his disciple. Watters further informs us that Dharmagupta was also lodged in this Vihāra about A.D. 585, and that among the students from distant lands who came there chiefly for the study of the Vinaya was the famous Vimalākṣa, a contemporary of Kumārajīva [p. 64].

In the *Po-lu-ka* (Bālūkā, the sands) country were some tens of monasteries with above 1,000 brethren of the Sarvāstivādin school.

Next the pilgrim passes by countries under Turkish rule such as *Tushkend*, *Samarkand*, and *Tokhara*, with little traces of Buddhist influence, till he comes to *Termiz* with above ten monasteries and 1,000 brethren, and beautiful topes and images of the Buddha. There were a few other places in the neighbourhood with monasteries, but the best centre of Buddhism in that locality was *Kunduz* where Yuan Chwang made the acquaintance of Dharmasaṅgha, a noted Hīnayāna scholar. The ruler of the place gave the pilgrim escort and 'post accommodation' (contributions of service imposed on subjects by government, such as supply of men and horses and accommodation for officials when travelling on duty) on his way southwards towards India, and asked him to visit *Balkh* (Fo-ho) as a Buddhist centre under his horde. Its capital itself was called 'Little Rājagṛiha City', with above 100 Buddhist monasteries and more than 3,000 brethren of Hīnāyāna school. Outside the capital was the Nava Saṅghārāma, 'the only Buddhist establishment north of the Hindukush, in which there was a constant succession of Masters who were commentators on the canon'. It had a costly image of Buddha and Vaiśravaṇa and other rarities, which made it a frequent object of plunder by the neighbouring barbarian chiefs. The monastery had also some relics of the Buddha—his washing basin, his tooth, and his broom—which were exhibited publicly on festival days, while there was a tope close by which also contained relics. There was a learned monk named Prajñākara in this monastery, with whom Yuan Chwang studied certain Abhidharma treatises and the Vibhāṣāśāstra.

Leaving *Balkh*, he came to the country of *Gaz*, with more than ten monasteries and 300 monks of the Sarvāstivādin school, to *Bamian*, with tens of such monasteries and several thousands of monks of the Lokottaravādin school, and to *Kapisa* on the confines of India, which, as we have already seen, was an important centre of Buddhism, with its monasteries numbering more than 1,000, and its monks, chiefly Mahāyānists, more than 6,000.

On his return journey by a different land-route, Yuan Chwang found centres of Buddhism in the following places: *Tsao-ku-t'a* with its capital Ghazni, which had hundreds of monasteries and above 10,000 Mahāyāna monks, the country of *Kabul* under a Turkish king who was a zealous Buddhist; *Andarab* in Tokhara country which, though Turkish, had a few monasteries and monks, including an Asokan tope, the country of *Khost*; *Badakshan*, with a few monasteries and under a king who had a 'profound belief in Buddhism'; *Kuran*, similarly under a king of Buddhist leanings; *Wakhan* with above ten monasteries, one of which had a stone image of the Buddha under a gilt-copper canopy set with precious stones; *Tashkurghan* (in the Pamir valley) where the people were 'sincere Buddhists', the reigning king, 'a patron of Buddhism and a scholar of culture', one of whose ancestors, according to tradition, was subdued by Asoka who built a tope in his palace there, whereupon he removed to another place where he erected a splendid monastery for the śāstra-master Kumāralabdha, forcibly brought to this land from his native place of Taxila, who was the founder of the Sautrāntika school and ranked with Aśvaghosa in the east, Deva in the south, Nāgārjuna in the west, the great Buddhist luminaries; *Osh*, with more than ten monasteries and 1,000 monks of the Sarvāstivādin school; *Kashgar*, with hundreds of monasteries and monks who memorized the entire Tripiṭaka and the Vibhāṣās or Commentaries without studying much their meanings, where the writing was also borrowed from India; *Che-ku-ka* which had a larger number of Mahāyāna texts 'than any other country to which Buddhism had reached'; and, lastly, *Khoten* (Sans. Gosthāna, or Kustana), where Yuan Chwang found the Indian system of writing, the people as Buddhists, above 100 monasteries with more than 5,000 monks, chiefly Mahāyānists, and the reigning king also a Buddhist; also varieties of Buddha images, and monasteries associated with Vairochana and Yaśas (' the great arhat in Asoka's time and the minister of Asoka who led a colony to Khoten ') [Watters, ii. 302], and other traditions.

Thus we may reasonably state that, on the whole, India saw in the age of Harṣa one of the most glorious periods of her history, when internally she was efficiently organized for a free and full self-expression under a sovereign who was an unbending idealist, while, externally, she was thus enabled more effectively to impress her thought upon her neighbours who turned to her as the home of the highest wisdom and culture in those days.

According to the *Life* (p. 156), Harṣa died 'towards the end of the Yung Hui period', i.e. about A.D. 655, a date accepted by Takakusu [*I-tsing*, pp. lvi and 163]. But Chinese sources place the event in A.D. 648, as pointed out by Watters [i. 347], since that was the date when a usurper was found on the throne of Harṣa by the Chinese envoy deputed to his court. Besides, according to Watters, it was in that year, too, that Yuan Chwang submitted the records of his travel to Tai Tsung, and 'Śīlāditya must have been dead before this work was drawn up in its present form'.

Let us now conclude with an estimate of Harṣa's character as given in the eloquent words of his best biographer, Bāṇa: 'Through him the earth does, indeed, possess a true king! Wonderful is his royalty, surpassing the gods! His liberality cannot find range enough in suppliants, nor his knowledge in doctrines to be learned; his poetical skill finds words fail, as his valour lacks opportunities to exercise it; his energy wants scope and his fame sighs for a wider horizon; his kindly nature seeks in vain more hearts to win, his virtues exhaust the powers of number, and all the fine arts are too narrow a field for his genius.' It is difficult to describe more briefly and forcibly the different aspects of his supremely versatile genius and complex character. He was at once a prince and a poet, a warrior and a man of letters, royal and kindly, with unbounded wealth given away in unbounded liberality, with the dignity of a paramount sovereign joined to the humility of a beggar, master of all the military as well as the fine arts, of all knowledge and virtues. Beginning as a militarist under the then prevailing political circumstances of the times which forced on him a career of vengeance and violence, campaigns and conquests, he soon returned to his normal state, his true self, and remained as a confirmed pacificist throughout his long reign, the most distinguished follower and preacher of the creed of non-violence in that violent age of warring kingdoms, so that in the spirit of his great predecessor in the same creed, viz. Aśoka Maurya, he could thus speak of himself through the hero of his own creation [King Jīmūtavāhana of his *Nāgānanda*]:

स्वशरीरमपि परार्थे यः खलु दद्यामयाचितः कृपया ।
राज्यस्य कृते स कथं प्राणिवधक्रौर्यमनुमन्ये ॥

'He who is ready, of his own motion, unasked, to give his life for the good of others, out of sheer compassion for them—how can he even think of the enormity of himself killing his fellow human beings merely to win an earthly kingdom?' We need hardly say that in his actual history subsequent to his conquests we find very largely realized this lofty ideal laid down for kings.

INDEX

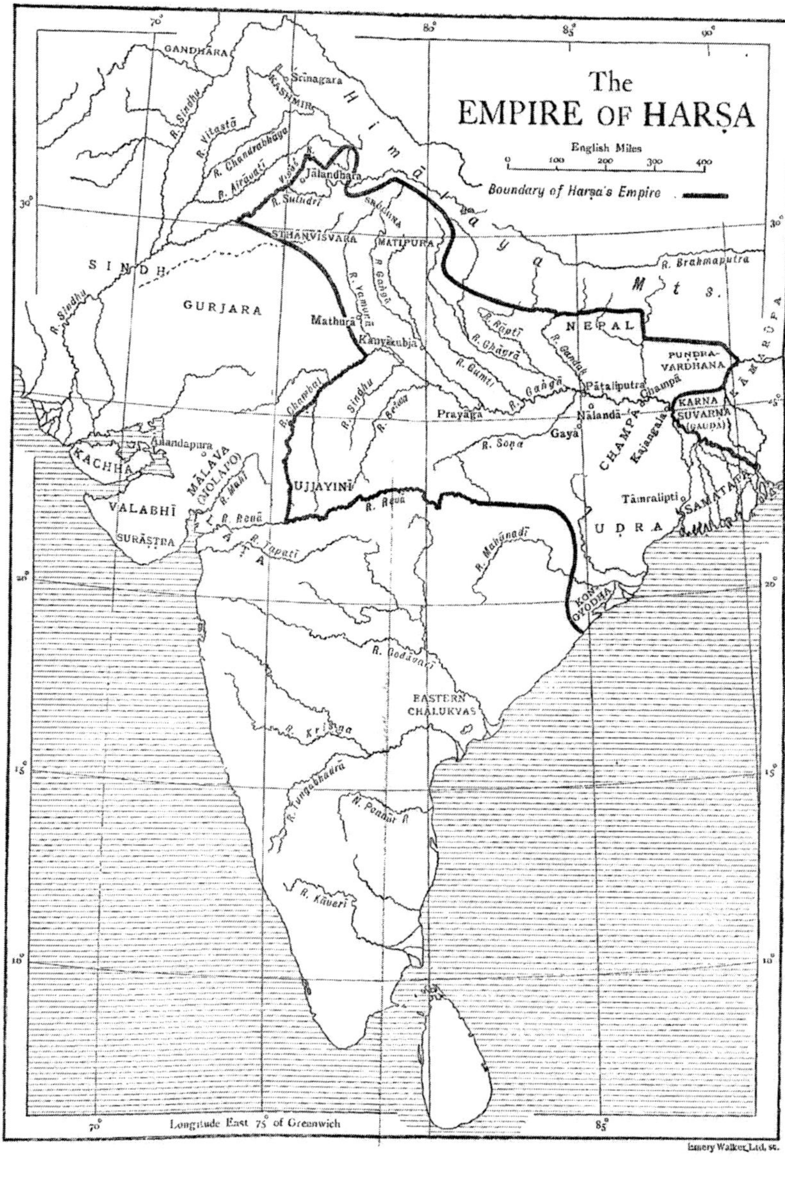

Emery Walker Ltd. sc.